Better Homes and Gardens ®

CHRISTMAS

❧ FROM THE HEART ®❧

Better Homes and Gardens ®

CHRISTMAS
❧ FROM THE HEART ®

VOLUME 9

Better Homes and Gardens Crafts Collection ™
Des Moines, Iowa

Contents

RED-AND-WHITE
Delights

As fresh as peppermint and as traditional as a

candy cane, red and white are surefire Christmas favorites.

On a bright bedroom tree (opposite), silver-framed redwork

ornaments inspired by the bed's quilt mingle with a paper

dove garland, felt ice-skate ornaments with paper-clip blades,

and glitter-covered balls. Under the tree, perky packages sport

felt-and-paper cutwork tags. Instructions begin on page 14.

There's a bit of Christmas magic in the reverse-appliqué ornaments (opposite) and pillow (below). Though they look complicated, the technique is simple. Machine-stitch together two contrasting layers of felt along the design lines, then snip away the excess top fabric to let the background show through. Trim the outside with pinking shears for sculptured edges. Add another layer of backing for the ornaments, or place four hearts on a pillow. Instructions begin on page 18.

Crown a plain frosted ornament with a glistening cap of glitter.

Simply brush the top of a purchased ornament with crafts glue, then

shake on a blizzard of white or clear glitter and let dry.

Tiny paper birdhouses joined in a row (opposite) lend a lighthearted

touch to a garland or tree. Paper doilies provide the roofs' lacy trim.

Instructions for the garland are on page 20.

Boxes this beautiful (opposite) are a gift on their own, no matter what's tucked inside. Embossed wallpaper provides the rich texture and needs little enhancement—just a sheer ribbon and some berries. These pears (below) are truly too pretty to eat. Plastic fruits, coated with sheets of silver leaf, are an elegant addition to any centerpiece. Instructions are on page 21.

PAPER DOVE GARLAND

Shown on pages 6–7.
The garland is 2½" tall.

YOU WILL NEED

Tracing paper
Ivory sketchbook paper
Rectangular paper doilies
Matte-finish adhesive tape
Black fine-tip permanent marking pen
Glue stick
Plain white paper

INSTRUCTIONS

Trace the dove and wing patterns onto tracing paper, and cut them out. Divide the ivory paper into 3¾"-wide sections, and fold it accordion style. Trace the dove pattern onto the first layer of ivory paper, aligning the left and right edges of the dove with the folded edges. Cut out the dove through all layers, being careful not to cut at the folds. Make additional garland sections as needed to achieve the desired length. To attach the sections, fold a 1" piece of tape over the top of the connecting area; trim the tape even with the bottom edges.

For each dove's wing, position the wing pattern at the corner of a doily, using a large scallop for the tip of the wing. Trace the wing pattern onto the doily, and cut it out. Glue the wing to the dove's body. Cut a sheet of plain paper into quarters; lay a quarter-sheet of paper over the wing. Press down on the paper to remove excess glue; change the paper as needed. Use the black marking pen to dot the eyes.

—Designed by Barb Vaske

PAPER DOVE GIFT TAG

Shown on pages 6–7.

YOU WILL NEED

Tracing paper
Ivory sketchbook paper
Rectangular paper doily
4½" length of 2½"-wide red velvet ribbon
3×4½" rectangle of card stock
Decorative-edge scissors
Glue stick
Fine-tip gold marking pen
Hole punch
String

INSTRUCTIONS

Trace the dove and wing patterns onto tracing paper, and cut them out. Trace the dove pattern onto the ivory paper; cut it out, trimming the beak into a point. Position and trace the wing pattern at the corner of the doily, using the large scallop for the end of the wing. Cut out the wing. Use decorative-edge scissors to trim the raw edges of the velvet ribbon. Center, and glue the ribbon on the card stock. Glue the dove to the ribbon and the wing to the dove's body. Use the gold marking pen to dot the eye. Punch a hole at the center top for the package tie. Thread a length of string through the hole, and knot the ends.

—Designed by Barb Vaske

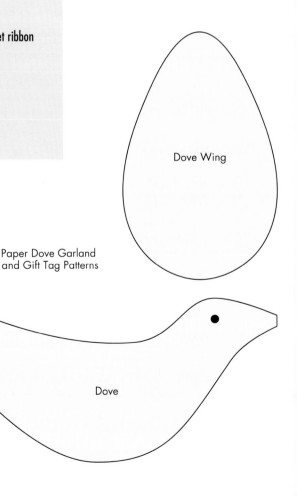

Paper Dove Garland
and Gift Tag Patterns

Dove Wing

Dove

REDWORK FRAMED ORNAMENTS

Shown on pages 6–7 and at right. The framed pieces range from 5½×4¼" to 7¼×6".

YOU WILL NEED

Tracing paper
White muslin
Water-erasable blue marking pen
Small embroidery hoop (optional)
DMC red (321) cotton floss
Embroidery needle
⅛"-diameter red buttons (optional)
Frames
Screw eyes
1"-wide ribbon
Florist's wire

INSTRUCTIONS

For each ornament, copy the desired pattern, *right* and *pages 16–17,* onto tracing paper. Cut a piece of muslin 2" larger than the design all around. Using a light source, trace the design onto the muslin with a water-erasable marking pen. Place the muslin in the embroidery hoop, if desired.

Outline-stitch with one ply of red embroidery floss. Use two plies of floss to satin-stitch and to make French knots and lazy-daisy stitches. If you prefer, sew on ⅛" red buttons in place of the French knots and satin stitches after the embroidery is complete.

To remove the marking pen lines, submerge the finished embroidery in cold water. Do not twist or wring it. Remove the fabric from the water, and lay it on a clean white towel. Pat the fabric with a dry towel. Smooth out the embroidery on another dry towel, and let it dry. Press, and frame as desired.

To hang the ornaments on a tree, insert an eye screw in the center top of each frame. Tie ribbon into a bow through the eye. Use florist's wire for hangers.

—*Adapted from antique designs*

Anchor		DMC
STEM STITCH		
9046	╱	321 Christmas red
SATIN STITCH		
9046	⬭	321 Christmas red
FRENCH KNOT		
9046	○	321 Christmas red
LAZY DAISY		
9046	⬭	321 Christmas red
SURFACE ATTACHMENTS		
	⊙	⅛"-diameter red button

Redwork Framed Ornament Pattern

RED-AND-WHITE DELIGHTS

Redwork Framed Ornament Patterns

Redwork Framed Ornament Patterns

Anchor   DMC
STEM STITCH
  9046 ╱ 321 Christmas red
SATIN STITCH
  9046 ◐ 321 Christmas red
FRENCH KNOT
  9046 ○ 321 Christmas red
LAZY DAISY
  9046 ◊ 321 Christmas red
SURFACE ATTACHMENTS
       ⊙   ⅛"-diameter
            red button

away the white felt approximately 1/16" beyond the stitching lines. At the bottom of the heart, cut three extended teardrops in the diamond shape. Use the pinking shears to trim away the white felt 1/4" beyond the stitching lines of the large heart.

Center the stitched piece, right side up, on the second piece of red felt; pin together. Thread your sewing machine with red thread. Sew just beyond the pinked edges of the large white heart shape. Use the pinking shears to trim away the red felt layers approximately 1/4" beyond the pinked white felt edge.

For a hanging loop, fold the 9" length of braid in half. Sew the braid ends to the back of the ornament at the top center.

—*Designed by Alice Okon*

REVERSE-APPLIQUÉ FELT WORK PILLOW
Shown on pages 7–9 and at left.

YOU WILL NEED
13" square of tracing paper
2—13" squares of red felt
1—13" square of white felt
Dressmaker's tracing paper
Sewing thread: red and white
Sharp embroidery scissors that cut to a point
Pinking shears
1½ yards each of 1/4"-diameter white and 1/2"-diameter red sew-in twisted cording
12" pillow form or polyester fiberfill

INSTRUCTIONS
Diagonally fold the 13" square of tracing paper twice. Crease along the folds to form a large X when the paper is unfolded. Use the creases as a placement guide.

Place tracing paper over the pattern so a crease runs through the center

REVERSE-APPLIQUÉ FELT WORK ORNAMENTS
Shown on pages 7–9 and above.
The finished ornament is 4¾×5¾".

YOU WILL NEED
Note: *Directions are for the red ornament. Reverse the felt and thread colors to make the white ornament.*
Tracing paper
3—5×7" pieces of red felt
3—5×7" pieces of white felt
Dressmaker's tracing paper
Sewing thread: red and white
Sharp embroidery scissors that cut to a point
Pinking shears
9" length each of red and white braid

INSTRUCTIONS
Trace the pattern onto tracing paper. Center the pattern on one piece of red felt, and transfer the black pattern lines using dressmaker's tracing paper.

Center the red felt, pattern side up, on the white felt; pin the pieces together. Thread your sewing machine with white thread, and set the stitch length to 16 stitches per inch. Sew through both layers of felt on the transferred pattern lines. Begin sewing at the center of the design, and work toward the edges, completing the large outside heart last. Pull all the threads to the red felt side; knot and trim.

Turn the stitched piece over to work from the white-felt side. Referring to the photograph, use embroidery scissors to carefully cut of the heart, and the bottom of the white heart is ⅝" from the center of the X. Trace only the dashed stitching lines of the heart pattern onto the tracing paper four times, one heart over each crease.

Trace the diamond pattern onto the tracing paper between the hearts to complete the pattern. Center the completed pattern on one red felt square, and transfer the pattern lines using dressmaker's tracing paper.

For the pillow front, center the red felt, pattern side up, on the white felt; pin them together. Thread your sewing machine with white thread, and set the stitch length to 16 stitches per inch. Sew through both layers of felt on the transferred pattern lines. Begin sewing at the center of the design and work toward the edges. Pull all of the threads to the red felt side; knot and trim.

Turn the stitched piece over to work from the white felt side. Referring to the photograph on *page 9*, use the embroidery scissors to carefully cut away the white felt inside the stitching lines of the large heart shapes and outside the large diamonds, cutting approximately ¹⁄₁₆" from the lines. Use the pinking shears to trim away the white felt ¼" beyond the stitching lines of the large hearts. Cut three extended teardrop shapes in each of the diamond shapes, using the photo as a guide.

Use a ½" seam allowance to baste the ¼" white cording around the outside edges of the stitched pillow front, clipping the cording's seam allowance at the corners and

overlapping the ends at the center bottom. Baste the ½" red cording to the pillow front in the same manner.

Pin the pillow front, right side down, on top of the second red felt square. Sew the pillow front to the back, leaving an opening to insert the pillow form. Clip the corners, trim the seam allowances, and turn the pillow right side out. Insert the pillow form, or stuff firmly with polyester fiberfill. Hand-sew the pillow opening closed.

—*Designed by Alice Okon*

Pillow Diamond Pattern

Reverse-Appliqué Felt Work Patterns

ICE-SKATE ORNAMENTS

Shown on pages 6–7 and at left.
The finished ornament is 3" tall.

YOU WILL NEED

Note: *These materials will make six ornaments*
6×14" piece of red felt
Tracing and transfer paper
6" square of lightweight cardboard
Polyester fiberfill
18" length of white lace trim
6 large paper clips
Black embroidery floss
24" length of ¼"-wide red satin ribbon

INSTRUCTIONS

Copy the skate pattern onto tracing paper, and transfer it onto the cardboard. Cut out the shape with scissors. Fold the felt piece lengthwise to measure 3×14". Lay the cardboard pattern on the felt, and trace around the shape with a fine-point pen, transferring six shapes. Stitch around the drawn shapes just inside the traced lines, leaving the tops of the skates open. Cut out the shapes, and stuff them with fiberfill. Sew the lace trim around each skate ornament opening.

Slide a paper clip into each skate, carefully creating an opening with scissor tips if necessary.

Lace the skates with two strands of black embroidery floss, and tie the ends in a bow. Sew on a 4" ribbon loop for hanging.

—*Designed by Ann Blevins*

BIRDHOUSE GARLAND

Shown on page 11.
The garland is 4" tall.

YOU WILL NEED

Tracing paper
Ivory sketchbook paper
Large-hole paper punch
4" paper doilies
Matte-finish tape
Glue stick
Plain white paper

INSTRUCTIONS

Trace the birdhouse pattern onto tracing paper, and cut out the pattern piece. Divide the ivory paper into 2¼"-wide sections and fold accordion style. Trace the birdhouse pattern onto the first layer of ivory paper, aligning the left and right edges of the birdhouse with the folded edges. Cut out the

Birdhouse

Birdhouse Garland Pattern

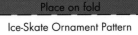

Place on fold

Ice-Skate Ornament Pattern

birdhouse through all layers, being careful not to cut at the folds. Make additional sections as needed to achieve the desired garland length. To attach garland sections, apply tape at the roof and birdhouse ledge on the back side of the garland. Use the paper punch to make a hole in each birdhouse 1⅛" from the bottom edge.

Cut ¾"-wide strips from all edges of the doilies. Glue a strip to each side of the roof, starting at the bottom of the roof and overlapping at the top. Position the strips to extend beyond the top edges of the birdhouse. Divide the plain white paper into quarters; lay a quarter-sheet of paper over the doily. Press down on the paper to remove excess glue; change the paper as needed. Working from the back side of the birdhouse, trim off the doily that extends beyond the roof line.

—*Designed by Barb Vaske*

TEXTURED WALLPAPER BOX

Shown on page 12.

YOU WILL NEED

Papier-mâché box
Textured wallpaper
Tape measure
Crafts glue and dish
2" sponge brush

INSTRUCTIONS

Place the box lid, top side down, on the wrong side of the wallpaper. Use a pencil to trace around the lid. Cut out the lid shape, adding a ½" margin for the tabs. Use a tape measure to determine the circumference of each lid; add ½" for overlap. Measure the height of the lid; add ⅛". Use these

measurements to cut a strip of wallpaper for the sides of the lid.

Place the box base on the wrong side of the wallpaper. Trace around the base; cut on the traced line. Use a tape measure to find the circumference of the base; add ½" for overlap. Measure the height of the base; add 1" for top and bottom tabs. Use these measurements to cut a piece of wallpaper for the base sides.

Mix glue and a few drops of water in a dish until the glue is the consistency of light cream. Lay the box-lid wallpaper shape, right side down, on a covered work surface. Use a sponge brush to apply an even coat of diluted glue to the paper shape, beginning at the center and working out to the edges. Center the piece of glued paper on the lid, smoothing from the center out. Fold the margins down onto the lid sides, using scissors to clip a tab every 1".

For the lid sides, apply glue to the wallpaper strip and press the strip onto the lid sides, letting the strip extend ⅛" beyond the lid bottom.

Apply glue to the wallpaper for the box base sides. Press the glued paper onto the base sides, keeping an even margin of paper at the top and bottom for the tabs. Fold the margins into the box at the top and onto the bottom of the base, clipping a tab every 1". Apply glue to the box-base shape; center the shape on the bottom of the base, smoothing from the center out. Place the lid on the base and let the glue dry.

—*Designed by Barb Vaske*

SILVER-LEAFED PEARS

Shown on page 13 and above.

YOU WILL NEED

Plastic pears with stems
100-grit sandpaper
Aleene's Metallics: Silver (303)
Paintbrush: medium flat
Silver die-cut leaves
2 ounces gold leaf adhesive
Silver leaf in a 25-sheet package
Soft brush
Spray sealer

INSTRUCTIONS

Sand the pears lightly to degloss the surfaces. Paint the pears with one or two coats of silver paint, allowing the paint to dry between coats. Also paint the leaf stems and the backs of the leaves silver.

Apply gold leaf adhesive to the pears. Let the adhesive set for about 30 minutes until it is tacky. Apply silver leaf over the adhesive; brush off the excess with a soft brush. Seal the pears with a clear protective sealer, following the manufacturer's directions. Wrap the stem of a leaf around the stem of each pear.

—*Designed by Dawn Anderson*

HOLIDAY
Garlands
AND
Wreaths

The classic shapes of gentle swags and never-ending circles grace mantels, stairways, walls, doors, and tables every holiday season. This year, craft your garlands and wreaths from unexpected materials. A chicken-wire frame packed with baubles and bows (opposite) showcases vintage, collectible, or new ornaments in a cheery, colorful way and can be made to fit almost any space. Instructions are on page 29.

Red winter roses add rich color to brilliant preserved oak leaves
(above), offering a slightly new take on traditional red and green.
Use the diminutive ring around a candle or in any small space.
Three concentric circles—copper-painted ruscus, gold-sprayed eucalyptus,
and green princess pine—form a luxurious wreath that goes
together quickly. Instructions are on page 29.

Bands of ribbon and strands of beads cascade along a
banister (above), falling in graceful twists and turns. A cluster of
pinecones anchors each point where the ribbon ties to the rail.
A purchased or homemade juniper wreath plays host to dark red
cockscomb, woodroses, and bunches of bright green grapes (opposite).
Instructions are on page 29.

Holly leaves joined end-to-end with tiny jingle bells drape
across the backs of chairs, framing the dining table in a fun but subtle way.
Narrow ribbon and a tiny ornament complete the jolly look.
For comfort, snip the prickly ends from the holly leaves before stringing
them into the swag. Instructions are opposite.

HOLLY GARLAND
Shown opposite.

YOU WILL NEED

30 holly leaves
30 — ³⁄₁₆" silver jingle bells
1 yard each of ¼"-wide red and ⅛" ivory ribbon
Christmas ornament
Needle and green thread

INSTRUCTIONS

With needle and thread, overlap two leaves and a bell, and sew together. Continue joining the leaves and bells to create two lengths of six leaves, and two lengths of nine leaves. Sew each short strand to a long strand. Tie three red bows and sew them to the center and the ends. Sew the ornament and the ivory bow to the center bow.

ORNAMENT SWAG
Shown on pages 22–23.

YOU WILL NEED

Chicken wire
Felt
6 yards of ribbon (for ends)
65 to 75 ornaments
Plastic-coated wire
Assorted ribbons (for fill)
Glue gun and hotmelt adhesive

INSTRUCTIONS

Cut out a swag shape from the chicken wire and the felt. Tie a ribbon bow at each end, and hang to have access to the back of the swag.

Hot glue the ornament caps to the ornaments. Attach a 4"-piece of wire to each ornament, then twist onto the swag, starting in the center, and working outward. Fill empty areas with ribbon bows. Hot glue the felt to the back of the swag.

ROSES AND OAK LEAF WREATH
Shown on page 24.

YOU WILL NEED

Preserved lime-green oak leaves
5" wire frame
String
9 freeze-dried red roses
Glue gun and hotmelt adhesive

INSTRUCTIONS

Tie a 24" piece of string to the wire frame. Cut the leaf stems to 5" and 6" lengths. Gather a few leaves and tie to the frame with the string. Continue tying groups of leaves until all the string is used. Tie another string to the frame and add leaves until the frame is covered. Use hotmelt adhesive to apply additional leaves to sparse areas. Glue the roses to the wreath with hotmelt adhesive.

PRINCESS PINE WREATH
Shown on page 25.

YOU WILL NEED

12" wire wreath form
Fresh princess pine pieces
Gold gunni eucalyptus
Copper ruscus
String
3 yards of 3"-wide wire edged ribbon

INSTRUCTIONS

Trim the materials to lengths of 3 to 4". Tie a 24" piece of string to the frame. Wrap bundles of ruscus around the frame. Continue around the frame with a band of eucalyptus and then pine, adding string when needed. Tie the wire-edge-ribbon into a bow and tie to the wreath.

WOODROSES WREATH
Shown on page 26.

YOU WILL NEED

20" juniper wreath
6 woodroses
Dried red cockscomb celosia
Artificial grapes
2 yards of ribbon
Fine-gauge wire

INSTRUCTIONS

Hot glue the woodroses, celosia, and grapes to the wreath in a pleasing arrangement. Cut lengths of ribbon of varying sizes from 3 to 6". Wrap wire around each ribbon end. Hot glue the wired ribbon ends into the wreath so the ribbon appears to be woven through the wreath. Tie a large ribbon bow and hot glue to the wreath.

RIBBON GARLAND
Shown on page 27.

YOU WILL NEED

Plastic-coated wire
9 large pinecones
10 rolls of ribbon

INSTRUCTIONS

Twist a wire length around the banister rail at the top, middle, and bottom, leaving 10" ends. At the top of the banister attach the ribbon ends to the wire. Twist the ribbons down the banister. Gather the ribbon, creating a swag shape, and wire it to the banister at the center and the bottom. Trim the ribbon ends. With wire, assemble groups of three pinecones and a large ribbon bow. Attach each arrangement with wire to the center and ends of the banister.

—All projects designed by Lorna Call

WELCOME, *Santa!*

Set the stage for the arrival of the Jolly Old Elf with a table setting (opposite) that celebrates gift-giving. Place mats shaped like oversize tags and a photo-filled topiary will get everyone in a festive mood. Then fill the house with other salutes to Santa—a cross-stitch picture and embroidered pillow, a painted candlestick, and a quilt-robed doll. Send Santa on his way with a mug of Good-Night Cocoa garnished with a peppermint stick. The recipe and project instructions begin on page 36.

The cross-stitched Santa (opposite) reminds us all to be jolly at this time of year by flying the phrase from his staff. There's no need to custom-frame this piece; it fits a standard 5×7-inch frame. A crown of berries gives this porch-post Santa (right) a European look and adds elegance to a holiday display. Trace the pattern onto a turned wooden post, then follow our easy painting directions to create the candlestick. Instructions begin on page 38.

Get out the crayons—then color our tiny embroidered pillow (above).

French knots and backstitching finish the design.

A patchwork coat keeps this bearded fellow (opposite) warm and cozy

during his midnight ride. Piece the fabric in two large blocks, then

cut and sew the jacket pieces. Instructions begin on page 42.

GOOD-NIGHT COCOA

Shown on pages 30, 94, and 100.

YOU WILL NEED

- 2½ cups nonfat dry milk powder
- 1½ cups tiny marshmallows
- 1 cup sifted powdered sugar
- ½ cup powdered nondairy creamer
- ½ cup unsweetened cocoa powder
- 1 tablespoon ground cinnamon (optional)

INSTRUCTIONS

Stir together milk powder, marshmallows, powdered sugar, nondairy creamer, cocoa powder, and if desired, cinnamon. Place in an airtight container, and store at room temperature for up to 3 months. For each serving, stir together ⅓ cup cocoa mix and ¾ cup boiling water in a mug.

GIFT-TAG PLACE MATS

Shown on page 31.
The place mat measures 12×16".

YOU WILL NEED

- 12×16" canvas artist's board
- Utility knife or scrollsaw
- 100- and 150-grit sandpaper
- Paintbrushes: ¾" flat, 1" stencil brush, and 2" sponge brush
- Delta Ceramcoat Acrylic colors: Burnt Sienna 2030 (BS), Cardinal Red 2077 (CR), Green Isle 2008 (GI), and Light Ivory 2402 (LI)
- ¾"-wide masking tape
- Tracing paper
- Acetate
- X-ACTO knife or scrollsaw
- Matte-finish varnish
- Medium-point permanent black marker
- Grommet tool and 1" grommet
- 26" of clothesline string

INSTRUCTIONS

Cut off two corners of the canvas board with a utility knife or scrollsaw. Sand the cut edges with 100- and then 150-grit sandpaper. Press two rows of masking tape around the perimeter of the board. Using a sponge brush, basecoat all surfaces with LI, letting the paint dry between the coats. Let the paint dry and carefully remove the tape to create a border. Paint the border with two coats of CR.

Trace the pattern onto tracing paper. Lay the acetate over the traced pattern and cut out the design with the X-ACTO knife.

Using the stencil brush, stencil the "TO" and "FROM" with BS. Then stencil the leaves GI and the berries CR. Let the paint dry. Brush on varnish and let it dry. Write the names on the tag with the marker. Insert the grommet following the manufacturer's instructions. Loop the clothesline through the grommet and tie it in an overhand knot.

—Designed by Martha Sutyak

PHOTO-SPIRAL CENTERPIECE

Shown on page 31 and below left.
The spirals are 10" tall.

YOU WILL NEED

- Clay pot
- Paintbrush: 1" sponge brush
- Delta Ceramcoat Acrylics: Light Ivory 2401 (LI) and Napthal Red Light 2409 (NR)
- Satin-finish varnish
- Tan paper-covered wire

INSTRUCTIONS

Paint the pot rim LI and the pot NR; let the paint dry. Apply two coats of varnish, allowing ample drying time between coats.

For the spirals, shape the circle ends as shown in the photo, leaving a 10" end for the plant pokes.

—Designed by Martha Sutyak

Gift-Tag Place Mats Patterns

WELCOME, SANTA!

"BE JOLLY" CROSS-STITCH SANTA

Shown on page 32.

YOU WILL NEED

8×10" piece of 14-count Fiddler's Lite Aida cloth
Cotton embroidery floss
Desired frame

INSTRUCTIONS

Center and stitch the design on the Aida cloth. Use three plies of floss unless otherwise specified in the key. Press the stitched piece from the back. Frame as desired.

—Designed by Robin Kingsley

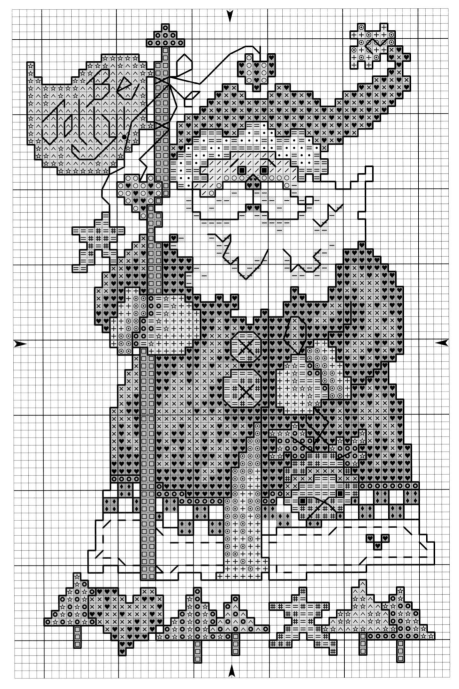

Anchor		DMC
002	⊡	000 White
1049	▣	301 Mahogany
979	◈	312 Navy
011	✕	350 Medium coral
923	◉	699 Dark Christmas green
227	☆	701 True Christmas green
257	∧	703 Chartreuse
305	▤	725 Topaz
868	╱	754 Peach
307	▦	783 Christmas gold
140	✛	813 Powder blue
047	♥	817 Deep coral
161	◎	826 Bright blue
381	■	938 Coffee brown
025	◯	3326 Rose
1031	▭	3753 Antique blue

BACKSTITCH

| 381 | ╱ | 938 Coffee brown – string on jingle bell and lettering (2X), all other stitches (1X) |

STRAIGHT STITCH (1X)

| 381 | ╱ | 938 Coffee brown – buttons, design on bottom of coat |

FRENCH KNOT

| 381 | ● | 938 Coffee brown – lettering (2X wrapped once) |

Stitch count: 85 high x 54 wide
Finished design sizes:
14-count fabric – 6 x 3⅞ inches
16-count fabric – 5⅓ x 3⅓ inches
18-count fabric – 4¾ x 3 inches

SANTA CANDLESTICK
Shown on page 33.

YOU WILL NEED

3¼×16¼" wooden turned post
100- and 150-grit sandpaper
Tack cloth
Wood sealer
Tracing and transfer paper
Paintbrushes: #12 flat, #8 flat, #3 round, #0 liner, ½" synthetic rake, and 1" sponge brush
DecoArt Americana Colors Acrylic Paint: Antique Teal DA158 (AT), Bluegrass Green DA47 (BG), Brilliant Red DA145 (BI), Country Blue DA41 (CB), Flesh Tone DA78 (FT), Light Avocado DA108 (LA), Lamp Black DA67 (LB), Napa Red DA165 (NP), Prussian Blue DA138 (PB), Pansy Lavender DA154 (PS), Red Violet DA140 (RV), Tangelo Orange DA196 (TN), and Titanium White DA1 (TW)
DecoArt Dazzling Metallics: Glorious Gold DA71 (GG)
Krylon 1311 Matte-Finish Spray
Matte-finish varnish
Antiquing medium

INSTRUCTIONS

Note: *Project designer Della Wetterman used an old salvaged post. After removing the loose paint, she sanded it and filled badly gouged areas with wood filler.*

Duplicate the patterns on *pages 40-41,* with tracing paper. Sand all surfaces with 100- and then 150-grit sandpaper. Remove the sanding dust with a tack cloth. Apply wood sealer to all surfaces, and let it dry. Sand again with 150-grit sandpaper, and wipe clean with a tack cloth.

Base-coat and shade with #8 and #12 flat brushes. Fill in small shapes with a #3 round brush, and apply details with a #0 liner brush. Use a rake brush to paint Santa's beard and hair.

Base-coat the candlestick

Using a sponge brush, base-coat the sections; start at the top of the post, and work toward the bottom. Base-coat the top section AT, the second section GG, the third section NP, and the fourth section GG. Base-coat the fifth section, which includes the band that touches Santa's head and extends to the blue section, with NP. Base-coat the blue section CB, the next section GG, the red section NP, and the last section AT. Let the paint dry, and then spray lightly with Krylon 1311 Matte-Finish Spray. Let the spray dry, and transfer the main pattern lines with transfer paper. There's no need to copy the details yet—you'll base-coat over them.

Blueberries and leaves

Base-coat the leaves and stems LA and TW mixed 1:1. Add more TW to the mixture, dilute it with water to ink consistency and, using a #0 liner brush, paint the tendrils.

Base-coat the blueberries CB, and shade with CB and PB mixed 2:1. Float tints of NP and/or TW and BG mixed 1:1. Paint the blossom ends LB and, before the paint dries, pick up TW on the dirty brush and highlight. Highlight each berry with a TW dot.

Base-coat the larger berries with RV and NP mixed 2:1. Let the paint dry. Use the handle end of a small brush to apply dots of the base-coat color around the edges of the berries; these dots should overlap the edges. Let the dots dry. Using a stylus, apply smaller PS dots to the first dots, and then fill in the rest of the berries with PS dots. Allow some of the base-coat color to show through. Let the dots dry. Apply smaller dots of TW and PS mixed 1:1 to all of the previous dots. Remember

that each layer of dots must be smaller than the previous layer. Let the dots dry. Place a small TW highlight dot on six to eight of the dots on the right side of each berry. Vary the placement of the highlight dots.

Use a stylus to apply the small dot flowers; dot the petals with TW and the centers with TN.

Paint Santa

Base-coat Santa's face FT, and shade under the hair on his forehead with FT and NP mixed 3:1. Dilute the shading mixture with water to ink consistency, and paint the nose lines. Mix FT and BI 2:1, and paint the cheeks. Paint the whites of the eyes TW, the irises with TW and BG

mixed 1:1 plus a small amount of AT, and the pupils with LB. Dilute LB with water to ink consistency, and paint a line along the top of each eye. Base-coat the entire mouth area, including the lip, with NP. Paint the lip with FT and NP mixed 2:1. Highlight the pupils, the cheeks, the nose, and the lip with TW dots.

Santa Candlestick Patterns

Base-coat Santa's hair, beard, mustache, and eyebrows with TW and LB mixed 5:1. Float LB on Santa's coat under the beard. Using a rake brush and paint thinned with water to ink consistency, paint a second layer of hair with TW and LB mixed 3:1; use a liner brush on the eyebrows. In the same manner, paint the first highlight layer. Wipe the excess paint from the brush, then load the dirty brush with TW and a small amount of BG and paint additional highlights. Using a liner brush and TW thinned with water to ink consistency, paint individual hairs; extend them beyond the original base-coated areas.

Final details

Use GG to paint the band along the bottom of the post, all comma strokes, and the dots.

Varnish the post, and let the varnish dry. Apply antiquing medium and remove the excess, leaving more in the shaded areas. Let the antiquing medium dry. Apply another coat of varnish, and let it dry.

—*Designed by Della Wetterman*

Santa Candlestick Patterns

BELIEVE! SANTA PILLOW

Shown on page 34.
The pillow is 7×5½".

YOU WILL NEED

⅛ yard of tea-dyed muslin
Fabric scraps in assorted colors
Water-erasable pen
Crayons
⅛ yard of cotton batting
Small embroidery hoop
Cotton embroidery floss
⅔ yard of jute
Polyester fiberfill

INSTRUCTIONS

From the tea-dyed muslin, cut one 5½×4" rectangle. From the assorted colored fabric scraps, cut one 1½×5½" strip, one 1½×5" strip, one 1½×6½" strip, one 1½×6" strip, and one 7½×6" rectangle. *Note: All measurements include a ¼" seam allowance unless otherwise specified.*

With the right sides facing, sew the 1½"-wide strips to the muslin rectangle in the following order, pressing each seam allowance toward the colored strip. Sew the 1½×5½" strip to the bottom edge, the 1½×5" strip to the left edge, the 1½×6½" strip to the top edge, and the 1½×6" strip to the right edge.

Using a light source, trace the Santa pattern onto the muslin rectangle with a water-erasable pen. Referring to the photograph and the illustration for color placement, color the design with crayons. Position the muslin block, right side up, on top of a piece of 6×8" cotton batting, and place the layers in an embroidery hoop. Use two plies of embroidery floss to complete the

Anchor	DMC	
BACKSTITCH (2X)		
926		Ecru – beard and mustache, hat trim and cuffs
403	310	Black – sleigh runners and lettering
1014	355	Terra-cotta – hat and jacket
371	433	Chestnut – sleigh and sack
817	469	Avocado – trim on sack, vine on sleigh
306	3820	Straw – star
STRAIGHT STITCH (2X)		
926		Ecru – hat trim and cuffs
817	469	Avocado – leaves on vine
FRENCH KNOT		
926		Ecru – Santa's beard (2X wrapped once)
403	310	Black – Santa's eyes and buttons, lettering (2X wrapped once)
1014	355	Terra-cotta – holly berries (1X wrapped twice)

backstitches and French knots. Trim excess batting that extends beyond the pieced strips.

Pin the muslin block and 7½×6" rectangle together with the right sides facing. Cut two 12" lengths of jute for the pillow hanger, and insert the jute between the fabric layers with one end of each length along the top edge of the pillow. Sew the block and back together, catching the jute ends in the seam allowance at the top and leaving a 2"-wide opening. Turn the pillow right side out, and stuff firmly with polyester fiberfill. Slip-stitch the opening closed. Tie the jute ends together in a bow.

—Designed by Barri Sue Gaudet

PATCHWORK COAT SANTA DOLL
Shown on page 35.
The finished Santa is 20".

YOU WILL NEED
⅜ yard of muslin or tea-dyed muslin for body
¼ yard of black check for arms and legs
½ yard of green print for pants and
    jacket binding
1—7" square of red print for pants cuffs
8—⅛ yard pieces of assorted red,
    green, and brown prints for jacket
3—1½"-diameter buttons
Black permanent marker for eyes
Pink blush for cheeks
1-pound bag of fiberfill for stuffing
Glue gun and hotmelt adhesive
Wool for beard and hair
Miniature basket filled with greens and
    jingle bells

INSTRUCTIONS
Note: *Quantities specified are for 44/45"-wide, 100% cotton fabrics. All measurements include a ¼"-seam*

allowance unless otherwise stated. To make the best use of your fabrics, cut the pieces in the order given.

Enlarge the patterns, *page 45,* using graph paper; cut out the patterns.

For the Santa

From muslin, cut two of Pattern A for the body. Fold the black check fabric in half and cut two each of Patterns D and E from the folded fabric for a total of four arm and four leg pieces.

With right sides together, sew the muslin A body pieces together, using small stitches and leaving a 3" opening in the bottom edge for turning. Clip the curves and turn right side out. Stuff the body firmly with fiberfill. Slip-stitch the opening closed.

With right sides together, pair the black check D pieces and the black check E pieces. Stitch around the legs and arms, leaving the ends open for turning. Clip the curves and turn right side out. Stuff each leg and arm firmly to the stuffing line indicated on the patterns. Stitch across each limb on the stuffing line. Turn under the raw ends ¼" and stitch each arm and leg to the body at the placement marks.

Referring to Pattern A for placement, make Santa's nose by pinching about ¼" of the face; stitch in place.

Using the permanent marker, draw the eyes on the face. Brush blush on either side of the nose for cheeks.

For the pants

From the green print, cut two of Pattern B for the pants. From the red print square, cut two 3×7" strips for the cuffs.

With right sides together, sew together the green print B pieces along

the crotch seams as indicated in Diagram 1.

Diagram 1

For the cuffs, with right sides together, fold the two red print 3×7" strips in half lengthwise. Stitch a folded strip to the bottom edge of each leg. Fold the trim to the right side.

Refold the pants so the sewn seams are centered front and back; sew the inseam (see Diagram 2 on *page 44*).

Diagram 2

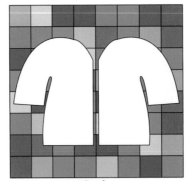

Jacket front

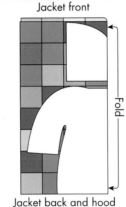

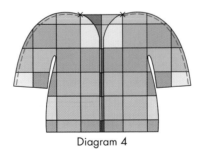

Jacket back and hood
Diagram 3

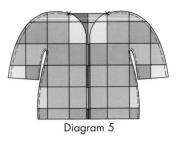

Diagram 5

Diagram 6

Turn under the waist edge of the pants. Using a double length of quilting thread, run a gathering stitch around the pants' waist edge. Leave the needle hanging loose and slip the pants on the Santa. Gather tightly around the Santa's waist and secure the thread.

For the patchwork
From the assorted red, green, and brown prints, cut 128—2½" squares. Lay out 64 of them in eight rows. Sew together the squares in each row. Press the seam allowances in one direction, alternating the direction with each row. Join the rows to complete a 16½" patchwork square, including the seam allowances. Press the seam allowances in one direction. Repeat to make a second patchwork square.

For the jacket
Referring to Diagram 3, from one piece of patchwork, cut one each of patterns F and F reversed for the jacket fronts. Fold the other piece of patchwork in half and cut one of Pattern F jacket back on the fold and one of Pattern C hood on the fold.

Use the remaining green pants print to cut one of Pattern C hood lining and two 3×42" strips for binding the jacket and hood.

With right sides together, join the patchwork front and back F pieces,

sewing from the shoulders to the wrists (see Diagram 4).

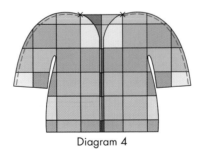

Diagram 4

Sew the side seam from the wrists to the jacket bottom edge (see Diagram 5).

Turn under the raw wrist edges ¼"; topstitch in place.

With right sides together, fold the patchwork C piece and the green print C piece in half. Stitch the back seam of each (see Diagram 6).

With wrong sides together, stitch together the hood front and lining at the neck edge with a gathering stitch.

Gently gather the edge of the hood to fit between jacket markings.

With right sides together, pin the hood to the jacket, matching hood center to the jacket center back and aligning raw edges; sew together.

With wrong sides together, fold one green print 3×42" strip in half lengthwise; press. Aligning raw edges, sew the binding to the right side of the jacket and hood, using a ¼"-seam allowance and sewing up the jacket front around the hood edge and down the other side of the jacket front. Turn the binding to the inside and hand-stitch in place. Use the remaining green print 3×42" strip to bind the lower edge of the jacket in the same manner, turning under the raw ends.

Put the jacket on the Santa. Overlap the front edges and pin. Stitch the three buttons to the jacket front, sewing through all layers.

To create a beard, add wool starting under Santa's nose and working out in layers; glue it in place as you work. Add layers of wool to the back and top of Santa's head and a small amount for his eyebrows. Pull the hood over Santa's head.

—Designed by Jean Lepper

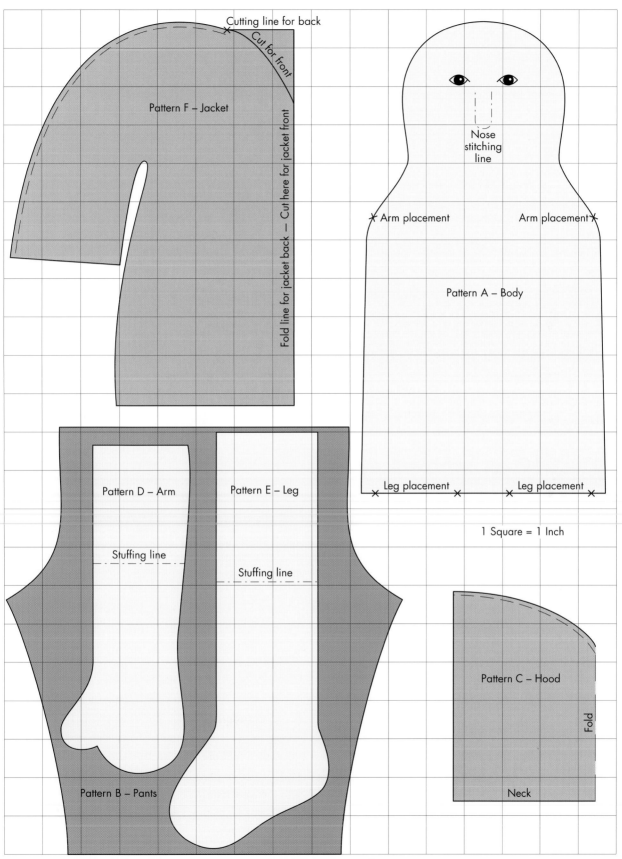

Cutting line for back

Cut for front

Pattern F – Jacket

Fold line for jacket back — Cut here for jacket front

Nose
stitching
line

Arm placement   Arm placement

Pattern A – Body

Pattern D – Arm   Pattern E – Leg

Stuffing line

Stuffing line

Leg placement   Leg placement

1 Square = 1 Inch

Pattern C – Hood

Fold

Pattern B – Pants   Neck

Patchwork Coat Santa Doll

GIFTS OF
Good Taste

The most cherished gifts are from the hands
and heart. This year, package your holiday breads,
jams, cookies, and candies in vintage containers gathered
at flea markets and garage sales. Fill tinware with
peppermint sticks (above), quick bread, and breakfast rolls
(left) to resemble gifts straight from Grandma's kitchen.
If you don't have time to bake, check out bazaars,
farmer's markets, and boutiques for locally made goodies.
The recipes for Mini Cinnamon Rolls and
Cranberry-Nut Bread are on page 52.

Cook up an old-fashioned treat to share in a time-tested container.
Add color by lining the container with a pretty napkin or square of country
fabric. Bar cookies and candies fit easily into a wooden crate. Recipes for Caramel
Corn (above), Peanut Butter Fudge, Brickle Bars, and Pistachio Cookie Sticks
(opposite top) are on page 53. For a clever presentation of purchased
truffles (opposite bottom), fill an antique muffin tin with toasted
and tinted coconut, then slip a candy into each cup.

Bridge the decades by packing contemporary treats in old-time containers.
Tuck a collection of holiday cookies into a '50s ornament box along with
some baubles from the era. The recipes for Mud Pie Cookies,
Cafe Brûlot Slices, and Spice Wafers are opposite.

MUD PIE COOKIES
Shown opposite middle.

YOU WILL NEED

¾ cup shortening
1½ cups sugar
⅔ cup unsweetened cocoa powder
2 teaspoons baking powder
1 teaspoon instant coffee crystals
2 teaspoons water
3 beaten eggs
1 teaspoon vanilla
2 cups all purpose flour
¼ cup finely chopped pecans
Mud Pie Frosting

INSTRUCTIONS

In a large mixing bowl beat the shortening with an electric mixer on medium speed for 30 seconds. Add sugar, cocoa powder, and baking powder; beat until combined. Dissolve the coffee crystals in water. Add coffee, eggs, and vanilla; beat until combined. Beat in as much flour as you can with the mixer. Stir in the remaining flour and pecans with a wooden spoon. Cover and chill for 1 to 2 hours or until the dough is easy to handle.

Shape the dough into 1" balls; place about 2" apart on an ungreased cookie sheet. Make an indentation with your thumb in the top of each cookie. Bake in a 375° oven for 8 to 10 minutes or until the edges are set. Cool on wire racks. Fill the centers with Mud Pie Frosting. Makes about 60 cookies.

Mud Pie Frosting: Beat ⅓ cup softened *butter* (no substitutes) and 1 teaspoon *vanilla* with an electric mixer on medium speed for 30 seconds. Slowly beat in ½ cup *unsweetened cocoa powder* and 1½ cups sifted *powdered sugar*; add 2 tablespoons *bourbon or milk*. Gradually beat in 1½ cups *powdered sugar* and enough *milk*

(1 to 3 tablespoons) to make a frosting of spreading consistency. Stir in ⅓ cup *miniature semisweet chocolate pieces.*

CAFE BRÛLOT SLICES
Shown opposite top.

YOU WILL NEED

1 cup packed brown sugar
½ cup pecan pieces
1 teaspoon instant coffee crystals
½ teaspoon ground cinnamon
¼ teaspoon ground cloves
½ cup butter (no substitutes)
1 tablespoon finely shredded lemon peel
1 tablespoon finely shredded orange peel
1 tablespoon brandy or milk
1 egg yolk
1¾ cups all-purpose flour
Brandy Icing

INSTRUCTIONS

In the bowl of a food processor combine the brown sugar, pecans, coffee crystals, cinnamon, and cloves. Cover and process until the nuts are finely chopped. Add butter, lemon peel, and orange peel; process until the butter is evenly mixed. Add brandy or milk and egg yolk; process until combined. Add flour gradually, processing until combined.

Divide the dough in half. Shape each half into a roll about 1½" in diameter and 6" long. Wrap and chill about 2 hours or until firm, or place in the freezer about 40 minutes.

Cut into ¼"-thick slices. Place the slices 1½" apart on an ungreased cookie sheet. Bake in a 375° oven for 7 to 8 minutes or until light brown. Transfer the cookies to wire racks to cool. Pipe or drizzle cooled cookies with Brandy Icing. Makes about 48 cookies.

Brandy Icing: Combine 1 cup sifted *powdered sugar*, ½ teaspoon *vanilla*, and 1 tablespoon *brandy or strong coffee*. Add *milk*, 1 teaspoon at a time, to make frosting of drizzling consistency.

SPICE WAFERS
Shown opposite bottom.

YOU WILL NEED

½ cup molasses
¼ cup packed brown sugar
¼ cup butter (no substitutes), melted
1½ cups all-purpose flour
½ teaspoon ground cinnamon
¼ teaspoon baking soda
¼ teaspoon ground ginger
¼ teaspoon ground cloves
¼ teaspoon pepper
⅛ teaspoon dry mustard
⅛ teaspoon ground allspice

INSTRUCTIONS

Stir together molasses and brown sugar in a large mixing bowl. Stir in melted butter. Stir in flour, cinnamon, baking soda, ginger, cloves, pepper, mustard, and allspice until well combined. Divide the dough in half. Cover and chill for 1 to 2 hours or until easy to handle.

Roll each portion of dough on a lightly floured surface to a ¹⁄₁₆" thickness. Cut with a floured 2" scalloped round cutter. Place on a greased cookie sheet. Bake in a 375° oven for 5 to 6 minutes or until light brown. Transfer to wire racks to cool. Makes about 66 cookies.

MINI CINNAMON ROLLS

Shown on page 46.

YOU WILL NEED

4 to 4⅓ cups all-purpose flour
1 package active dry yeast
1 cup milk
⅓ cup sugar
⅓ cup butter or margarine
½ teaspoon salt
2 eggs
¼ cup butter, melted
½ cup sugar
2 teaspoons ground cinnamon
Powdered Sugar Icing

INSTRUCTIONS

In a large mixing bowl combine 1½ cups of the flour and the yeast; set aside. In a medium saucepan heat the milk, the ⅓ cup sugar, the ⅓ cup butter, and the salt, stirring frequently until warm (120°–130°) and the butter almost melts. Add the milk mixture to the flour mixture along with the eggs. Beat with an electric mixer on low to medium speed for 30 seconds, scraping the sides of the bowl frequently. Beat on high speed for 3 minutes. Mix in as much of the remaining flour as you can stir with a wooden spoon.

On floured surface, knead in enough of the remaining flour to make a moderately soft dough that is smooth and elastic, 3 to 5 minutes total. Shape into a ball. Place in a greased bowl; turn once. Cover; let rise in warm place until doubled in bulk, about 1 hour.

Punch down the dough. Turn it out onto lightly floured surface. Divide the dough in half. Cover and let it rest for 10 minutes. In a small bowl, combine the ½ cup sugar and the cinnamon; set aside.

Divide each half of the dough in half again. Roll one portion into a 12×6" rectangle. Brush about 1 tablespoon of the melted butter on top of the dough and sprinkle with ¼ of the sugar and cinnamon mixture. Roll the rectangle, jelly-roll style, starting from one of the long sides. Pinch the seams to seal. Slice the dough into twelve 1" pieces. Place the pieces, cut side down, in greased muffin pans. Repeat rolling and shaping with the remaining portions of dough. Cover; let rise until nearly double (30 minutes). Or, cover with oiled waxed paper, then plastic wrap; refrigerate 2 to 24 hours.

If the rolls have been chilled, let them stand, covered, for 20 minutes at room temperature before baking. Puncture any surface bubbles with a greased wooden toothpick. Bake the rolls in a 375° oven for 10 to 12 minutes or until they test done. Cool slightly on a wire rack. Remove the rolls from the pans. Drizzle with Powdered Sugar Icing. Serve rolls warm or cool. Makes 48 miniature rolls.

POWDERED SUGAR ICING

YOU WILL NEED

2 cups sifted powdered sugar
½ teaspoon vanilla
About 2 tablespoons milk

INSTRUCTIONS

In a small mixing bowl combine the sifted powdered sugar, the vanilla, and enough milk to make a frosting of drizzling or spreading consistency. Makes about 1 cup.

CRANBERRY-NUT BREAD

Shown on page 46.

YOU WILL NEED

½ cup butter, softened
¾ cup sugar
1 egg
2½ cups all-purpose flour
1 tablespoon baking powder
1 teaspoon salt
⅔ cup orange juice
⅓ cup milk
¾ cup chopped fresh or frozen cranberries
1 teaspoon grated orange peel
½ cup chopped walnuts

INSTRUCTIONS

In a mixing bowl cream the butter and sugar until fluffy. Beat in the egg. Stir together the flour, baking powder, and salt. Combine orange juice and milk. Add the liquids alternately with the dry ingredients to creamed mixture, mixing well after each addition. Fold in the cranberries, grated orange peel, and half of the walnuts. Pour into one greased 8½×4½×2½" loaf pan or two greased 7½×3½×2" loaf pans. Sprinkle the top of the loaf or loaves with remaining walnuts. Bake the bread in a 350° oven, about 60 minutes for a large pan or 45 to 50 minutes for smaller pans. Cool the loaves in the pans for 10 minutes; remove the loaves from the pans. Cool completely. Makes 1 large or 2 small loaves.

CARAMEL CORN
Shown on page 48.

YOU WILL NEED

Nonstick spray coating
8 cups popped popcorn (⅓ to ½ cup unpopped)
¾ cup packed brown sugar
⅓ cup butter (no substitutes)
3 tablespoons light corn syrup
¼ teaspoon baking soda
¼ teaspoon vanilla

INSTRUCTIONS

Spray an 8×12×2" baking pan with nonstick spray. Remove unpopped kernels from the popped corn. Place the popcorn in pan; keep warm in a 300° oven.

Butter the sides of a heavy 1½-quart saucepan; add brown sugar, butter, and corn syrup. Clip a candy thermometer to the side of the pan. Cook and stir over medium heat to about 255°, hard-ball stage (about 4 minutes). Remove the saucepan from the heat. Stir in the baking soda and vanilla; pour the mixture over the popcorn. Stir gently to coat.

Bake in a 300° oven 15 minutes. Stir and bake for 5 minutes more. Remove the popcorn from the oven; spread onto foil and cool completely. Break into clusters. Makes 9 cups.

PEANUT BUTTER FUDGE
Shown on page 49 top.

YOU WILL NEED

4 cups sugar
2—5-ounce cans evaporated milk (1⅓ cups)
1 cup butter
1—10-ounce package peanut butter pieces
1—7-ounce jar marshmallow crème
1 cup finely chopped peanuts
1 teaspoon vanilla

INSTRUCTIONS

Line an 8×8×2" baking pan with foil; extend the foil over the edges of the pan. Butter the foil; set aside.

Butter the sides of a heavy 3-quart saucepan. In the pan combine sugar, milk, and butter. Cook and stir over medium-high heat until the mixture boils. Clip a candy thermometer to the side of the pan. Cook and stir over medium heat to 236°, soft-ball stage, about 12 minutes.

Remove the saucepan from the heat; remove the thermometer from the pan. Add the peanut butter pieces, marshmallow crème, peanuts, and vanilla; stir until the peanut butter pieces are melted. Spread into the prepared pan. Score into squares while warm. When firm, cut into squares. Store in the refrigerator. Makes about 3⅓ pounds (36 servings).

BRICKLE BARS
Shown on page 49 middle.

YOU WILL NEED

½ cup butter
2—1-ounce squares unsweetened chocolate
1 cup sugar
2 eggs
1 teaspoon vanilla
¾ cup all-purpose flour
¾ cup almond brickle pieces
½ cup miniature semisweet chocolate pieces

INSTRUCTIONS

In a medium saucepan melt the butter and unsweetened chocolate together over low heat, stirring frequently. Remove from the heat. Add the sugar, eggs, and vanilla. Using a wooden spoon, lightly beat just until combined (don't overbeat or the bars will rise too high, then fall). Stir in the flour.

Spread the batter into a greased 8×8×2" baking pan. Sprinkle with the almond brickle and the semisweet chocolate pieces. Bake in a 350° oven for 30 minutes. Cool in the pan on a wire rack. Cut into bars. Makes 16.

PISTACHIO COOKIE STICKS
Shown on page 49 bottom.

YOU WILL NEED

1¼ cups all-purpose flour
3 tablespoons sugar
¼ teaspoon ground cardamom
½ cup butter (no substitutes)
¼ cup finely chopped pistachios
½ cup semisweet chocolate pieces
1 teaspoon shortening

INSTRUCTIONS

In a medium mixing bowl stir together the flour, sugar, and cardamom. Using a pastry blender, cut in the butter until the mixture resembles fine crumbs. Stir in the pistachios. Form the mixture into a ball and knead until smooth.

On a lightly floured surface pat or roll the dough into a 10×6" rectangle. Bake in a 325° oven for 25 to 30 minutes or just until edges are light brown. While the dough is still warm, cut the rectangle into 3×1" sticks and remove from the pan. Cool the cookie sticks on wire racks.

In a small heavy saucepan melt the semisweet chocolate pieces and the shortening together over low heat, stirring occasionally. Drizzle the mixture over the cooled cookies. Makes 20.

DECK THE
Outdoors

You've decked the halls and trimmed the walls, hung
wreaths on the doors and so much more. Now spread
your cheer to the outdoor areas of your home. Whether
you're setting the stage for the arrival of guests, building a
snowman with the kids, treating wildlife to a tree of their
own, or simply pampering the family pooch, have fun
with your outdoor decorating scheme.

A FROSTY PICNIC BASKET
Turn that wooden barrel filled with nothing but dirt into an evergreen
"topiary" this winter. Bend heavy wire into a handle, and nail or staple it to a
wooden half barrel. Wrap and staple garlands of greenery around the barrel and
handle, and then tuck holly, clusters of pinecones, and other seasonal sprigs
between the garlands. Wire or staple the sprigs in place, and cover the dirt with
a generous mound of snow. Finally, fill your basket with apples, ears of corn, or
other tasty treats for the neighborhood wildlife.

TWEET TREATS

Trim a tree for the birds and squirrels this year (opposite). Spread stale bagel halves with peanut butter or honey, and coat them with birdseed. Hang them on the tree with twine, string, or yarn that the birds can use for springtime nests. Add ears of corn and apples for the squirrels and brightly colored bows to attract other wildlife. Finish the tree with garlands of cereal. The antics of neighborhood creatures will keep you entertained for weeks and help the critters make it through the long, cold winter.

WINTER GARDEN TRELLIS

Terra-cotta pots converted into candles and a flower-bell trellis take on the role of a wintry sculpture (right). Wedge a plastic-foam wreath inside a basket, placing it a few inches from the basket top. Slide the trellis in place, wiring where needed. Weight the basket with sand so it won't tip, and top it with pinecones. Sharpen the ends of evergreen sprigs, then insert them into the foam form to create a wreath that cascades over the basket. Shorten the ends of small torch-style outdoor candles. Slide the ends through the holes in the bottoms of terra-cotta pots and into the foam wreath. If torch-style candles aren't available, wire the pots securely in place and put a votive candle in each pot. Make sure the flames of the candles stay safely away from the greenery, trellis, and basket. Add a small bird's nest and some apples or other colorful trims.

SPRIGS-AND-TWIGS WINDOW BOX

Take an empty window box to new heights with a tall arrangement of greenery and berries. Use sand, pea gravel, or dirt to hold the elements in place. Starting with the taller, fuller items and working toward the smaller ones, create the arrangement just as you'd make a floral centerpiece. Add colorful sprigs of berries last. For our window box, we used an assortment of evergreens, variegated boxwood and privet, and red winter berries, but any combination of seasonal items would work as long as the colors and textures blend.

FRONT-YARD GREETINGS

Give friends and neighbors a chuckle when they pass by your home this winter. Just for fun, build a kiwi-eyed snowman out in the yard to beckon guests into the house. Mist him with water so he'll last a bit longer, and place a tiny tree in one arm for a colorful salutation. Wrap a thick swag of greenery around the front door, and stud it with lights and bows.

Let Heaven and Nature Sing

All the universe exhibits its splendor at this magical time of year, and it's even grander when brought indoors and embellished with a few simple trims. Pinecones wound with wire and iridescent marbles, beads that glimmer like icicles, and silken-winged dragonflies and butterflies grace our nature-inspired tree. Teacups tied to the branches hold tiny packages, adding still more sparkle.

Instructions begin on page 68.

Capture the delightful flight of dragonflies on an embossed velvet stocking (left). Use a rubber stamp and iron to emboss the pattern onto the fabric, creating a sophisticated tone-on-tone design. Beaded icicles topped with hair clips, dragonflies made from hot-melt adhesive and wire, and silver cups holding tiny packages (opposite) demonstrate how the simplest materials can become exquisite tree trims. Instructions begin on page 69.

The tree skirt (above), as soft and pristine as new-fallen snow,

buttons back to reveal embossed velvet on one side and a sheer leaf print

on the other. Crown packages with corsages of leaves, berries, and roses.

Silver teacups nestle in the gold-and-evergreen branches of this

centerpiece (opposite), lush with other mellow metallics—gilded pinecones,

shimmering berries, and silver, copper, and gold leaves.

Instructions begin on page 70.

Glistening snowflakes, silver and white candles in mismatched holders,

and snowball ornaments add touches of light to an arrangement of evergreens,

gold berries, branches, pinecones, leaves, and tiny white roses (above).

Silver teacups hiding votive candles provide the final twinklings of light.

A quintet of elaborate cut-paper ornaments depicts the Christmas story.

Cluster the finely detailed pieces together to grace a wreath, small tree,

or garland. Instructions begin on page 74.

HEAVENLY TREE

Shown on pages 60–61 and at left.

GENERAL INSTRUCTIONS

We used purchased gold pinecones and tree branches. If these aren't available, spray-paint fresh pinecones and branches. Lightly spray the leaves with gold, silver, or copper spray paint to enhance ivy and other garlands. Our snowball and snowflake ornaments also are purchased. You may substitute other ornaments.

YOU WILL NEED

Note: Depending on the size of your tree, you may need to adjust the quantities of the supplies and/or the number of ornaments you make.

7 strings of 100-count white lights
Large cardboard box
Florist's spray paint: gold, silver, and copper
3 bunches of gold tree branches
12 Teacup Arrangements (See page70)
Plastic-coated wire
12 Golden Pinecone Tree Corsages (opposite)
6 silk ivy garlands
12 silk rose heads
Purchased snowball ornaments
Purchased snowflake ornaments
Sparkling Icicle Ornaments (opposite)
Dragonfly Ornaments (See page 70)
20-gauge copper soldering wire

INSTRUCTIONS

To add extra color to a gold tree, color the tree-light cords by inserting the bulbs from the light strands into holes along the top cut edge of a large cardboard box. Then spray-paint the cord and bulb bases gold or a color that will complement your tree.

String the lights throughout the tree. Wire the gold branches to the tree with plastic-coated wire, spacing them evenly throughout. Tie on the Teacup

Arrangements; then attach the Golden Pinecone Tree Corsages to the tree. Fill in open areas on the tree by winding the ivy garlands throughout the tree. Wire the rose heads to the tree, spacing them evenly. Hang the snowball ornaments, and then the snowflakes to fill in dark areas. Hang the Sparkling Icicle and Dragonfly Ornaments on the outer branches. Finally, work the copper wire around and throughout the entire tree.

—Designed by Aubrey Dunbar

GOLDEN PINECONE TREE CORSAGE
Shown on page 60.

YOU WILL NEED
Silk rose leaves
Floral spray paint: silver
Metallic berry spray
4 or 5 white paper rosebuds
Brown floral tape
Copper Wire Spiral (right)
Large gold pinecone
20-gauge florist's wire

INSTRUCTIONS
Spray the rose leaves silver for the base of the corsage. Add a spray of berries and the rosebuds to the leaves. Tape everything together with floral tape. Attach the Copper Wire Spiral near the top of the corsage by wrapping the center of the ornament around the rosebud stems. Wrap florist's wire around the base of the pinecone, leaving a long tail. Attach the corsage to the pinecone by wrapping the tendril wire around the corsage stem. Use floral tape to wrap the tendril, and then curl the end.

—Designed by Aubrey Dunbar

SPARKLING ICICLE ORNAMENTS
Shown on pages 60–61, 63, and at right.
The finished icicles are 4" to 9" long.

YOU WILL NEED
Note: We list materials to make 12 ornaments.
Long beading needle
Spool of clear fishing line
1 small bag each of 12mm faceted crystal beads, 10×14mm silver-washed oval pony beads, 6mm lacquered copper round beads, 10.5mm antique copper corrugated rings, 10mm crystal sunburst beads, 25mm crystal sunburst beads, and 10mm opalescent sequins
2 bags each of 18×20mm acrylic crystal drops, 6×19mm silver spaghetti beads, and 6×19mm gold-washed spaghetti beads
3 bags of 26×51mm acrylic crystal bead drops
Assorted packages of tiny clear, copper-crystal, opalescent, and gold-crystal pebble beads
12 dragonfly or butterfly hair clips

INSTRUCTIONS
Thread the beading needle with fishing line, leaving the line attached to the spool. Slip assorted beads, rings, and sequins onto the fishing line until the icicle is the desired length. Add one of the crystal drops; then thread the needle back through all of the beads, rings, and sequins. Cut the fishing line, leaving 5" tails. Knot the tails together close to the cut ends. Thread the knotted tail through a hole in a dragonfly or butterfly hair clip, and tie several knots. Repeat to make additional ornaments.

—Designed by Laura Holtorf Collins

COPPER WIRE SPIRALS
Shown on pages 60–61 and 66.

YOU WILL NEED
20-gauge copper soldering wire
⅜"-diameter wooden dowel
Clear marbles

INSTRUCTIONS
For each ornament, cut an 18" or longer piece of copper soldering wire. Wrap approximately 6" of one end of the wire around the wooden dowel; remove the dowel. Repeat for the opposite end of the wire. Untwist some of the wire far enough to insert a marble; repeat for opposite end. Bend the center of the wire to attach to an ornament or tree branch.

—Designed by Aubrey Dunbar

LET HEAVEN AND NATURE SING

DRAGONFLY ORNAMENTS
Shown at right.

YOU WILL NEED

24-gauge gold spool wire
Needle-nose pliers
Wire cutters
Gold sheer fabric
Crafts glue
Scruffy brush
Small sharp scissors
Glue gun and gold glitter hotmelt
    adhesive sticks
Hotglue gun pad

INSTRUCTIONS

To make the wings, form a 10"-long piece of wire into a figure-eight shape, twisting the ends in the center. Repeat for the second set of wings. Tighten the wires with needle-nose pliers. Trim the ends with a wire cutter.

Brush glue on the wires, and sandwich each wire shape between two pieces of fabric. If necessary, lightly finger-press the fabrics onto the glue. Let the glue dry completely. Trim the wings by cutting the fabric away as close to the wire as possible.

For the dragonfly body, squeeze an elongated teardrop shape of glitter adhesive onto the glue gun pad. Let the glue cool, and peel off the shape. Referring to the photo, bend a 1" length of wire into antennae. Attach the wings, the antennae, and a 3" hanging wire to the underside of the body with hotmelt adhesive.

—*Designed by Ann Blevins*

TEACUP ARRANGEMENT
Shown below.

YOU WILL NEED

1 yard of ¾"-wide ribbon
Florist's wire
Silver tasseled cording
Spray of berries
2 to 4 white paper rosebuds
2 to 4 silver corsage leaves
Small silver cup

INSTRUCTIONS

Make a four-loop bow with ribbon. With the cording, tie a shoestring bow onto the four-loop bow. Attach the berry spray and the rosebuds. Attach 2 to 3 silver leaves to the base of the corsage. Wire the corsage to the base of the cup.

—*Designed by Aubrey Dunbar*

NATURAL-WONDER CENTERPIECE
Shown on page 64.

YOU WILL NEED

Ceramic or plastic shallow plate or bowl
Plastic foam
7 gold tree branches
6 large gold pinecones
Florist's wire
7 evergreen pine sprays
4 oak leaf sprays
Floral spray paint: gold, silver, and copper
4 metallic berry sprays
10 white paper rosebuds
2 Teacup Arrangements (left)

INSTRUCTIONS

Cut the plastic foam to fit in the bowl. Evenly insert the gold tree branches into the plastic foam. Wrap florist's wire around the base of each pinecone, leaving a tail. Insert the pinecones in the foam. Fill in the arrangement with evergreen pine sprays. Spray paint the oak leaves gold, silver, and copper. Insert the leaves around the base of the arrangement. Add the berry sprays and white rosebuds. Wire the cup corsages in the centerpiece arrangement.

—*Designed by Aubrey Dunbar*

BLANKET-OF-SNOW TREE SKIRT

Shown on page 65 and below. The finished tree skirt is 44" in diameter, including the fringe.

YOU WILL NEED

- 1⅓ yards of 45"-wide winter white rayon velvet
- Hot Potatoes Rubber Stamps: dragon fly stamps in three sizes
- Iron
- Teflon pressing cloth (optional)
- Spray bottle with water
- T-pin; chalk pencil
- 1 yard of string
- Yardstick
- 1⅓ yards of 45"-wide sheer leaf-print fabric
- 44" square of cotton batting or fleece
- 4¾ yards of 1¼"-wide beige fringe
- Matching sewing thread
- 2 large white hook-and-eye fasteners
- 2—2"-diameter self-cover button forms
- 8 assorted buttons, ranging from ½"- to 1⅜"-diameter

INSTRUCTIONS

Test the embossing method described below on velvet scraps; reserve the embossed scraps for the covered buttons. If steam holes show from the iron, use a Teflon pressing cloth.

Emboss the velvet

Cut a 44" square from the winter white velvet. Preheat the iron on the cotton setting. Lay the stamp on the ironing board with the rubber image up. Lay the velvet right side down on top of the stamp. Lightly mist the back of the velvet. Press the iron onto the velvet and stamp, using the part of the iron with no steam holes. Hold the iron steady over the design for 20 to 30 seconds, and lift the iron carefully. Continue embossing the dragonfly

images until you're satisfied with the design. Our dragonflies are approximately 2½" to 4" apart.

Cut the fabrics

For tree skirt front, fold the embossed velvet square in half with right sides facing. Find the center of the folded edge and mark it with a chalk pencil. Tie one end of a 22" length of string the T-pin and the other end to the pencil chalk. Anchor the T-pin to the mark on the folded edge. Draw a semicircle on the fabric with the chalk pencil by making an arc with the string (see the diagram *below*).

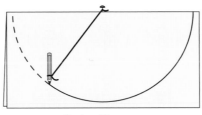

Cutting Diagram

For the tree-trunk opening, shorten the length of string between the chalk and the T-pin to 3"; make a semicircle. Cut through both layers of velvet on the marked lines. Unfold velvet with the wrong side up. Mark the center front opening, using a yardstick to draw a line from the center to the outer edge. Cut on the center front line.

Using the velvet front as a pattern, cut a similar piece from the sheer leaf-print fabric for the backing and another piece from the batting.

Sew the tree skirt

Pin the fringe to the outer edges of the circle, beginning with the center of the fringe at the center back of the velvet front. Continue the fringe around the corners and 11" up the straight edges at the center front; trim the excess

fringe. Baste the fringe in place.

Machine-baste together the batting and sheer backing fabric. With the right sides facing and the raw edges aligned, lay the velvet front and the backing together; pin them in place. Machine-sew the front and backing together along all the raw edges, leaving an opening for turning. Trim the seam allowance, and clip the curves. Turn the tree skirt right side out; finger-press the seams. Slip-stitch the opening closed.

For the lapels, fold back the front corners of the tree skirt so the backing shows; tack them in place. Sew hook-and-eye fasteners onto the backing side of the front opening, positioning one at the top and one just above the lapels.

Cover two buttons with the embossed velvet scraps, following the button manufacturer's instructions. Arrange the covered buttons and the remaining buttons on the lapels; sew them in place.

—*Designed by Laura Holtorf Collins*

DRAGONFLIES-IN-THE-SNOW STOCKINGS

Shown on pages 60–62, 74, and opposite.
The finished stockings are 18" long.

YOU WILL NEED:

For each stocking:
Graph paper
13×22" piece of winter white
   rayon velvet
13×22" piece of backing fabric
22×26" piece of cotton batting or fleece
1⅜ yards of decorative metallic cording
Matching sewing thread

For the Cuffed Stocking:
15×18" piece of sheer leaf-print fabric
10 — ½"- to 1"-diameter assorted buttons
Silver and gold metallic threads
Gold-tasseled curtain tieback

For the Dragonfly-Embossed Stocking:
Small dragonfly rubber stamp
Iron
Spray bottle with water
⅓ yard of sheer gold fabric
6 yards of ⅛"-wide ecru satin ribbon
8" length of ⅝"-wide sheer cream ribbon
Polyester fiberfill
6"-long corsage of white paper rosebuds,
   metallic berries, and silver leaves
Silver-tasseled curtain tieback

For the Leaf-Trimmed Stocking:
Assorted 5" to 10" lengths of wire-edge
   sheer metallic ribbons: 1"-wide copper,
   1½"-wide variegated copper-and-gold,
   2"-wide variegated silver-and-gold,
   and 2"-wide gold
Thin copper wire
Assorted metallic glass pebble and
   bugle beads
2 dragonfly barrettes
2—¾"-diameter rhinestone buttons

INSTRUCTIONS

Enlarge the stocking pattern on graph paper. Add ½" seam allowances beyond the drawn lines and cut out the completed pattern piece. Sew all pieces with right sides together using ½" seam allowances, unless otherwise noted.

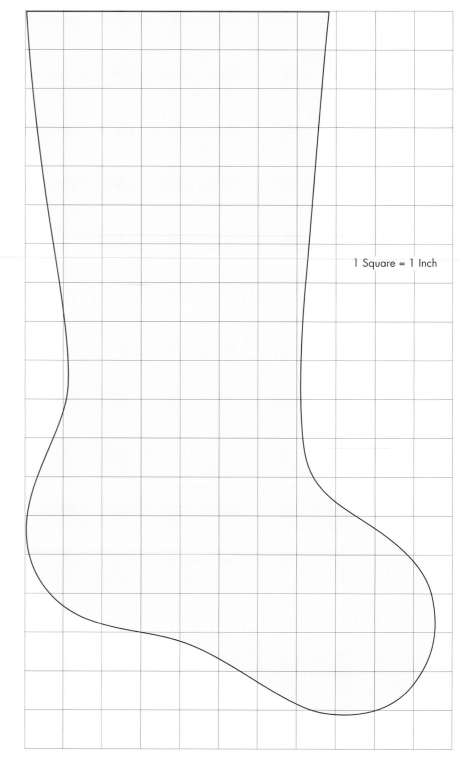

1 Square = 1 Inch

Stocking Pattern

Cut the Fabrics

For the Dragonfly Embossed Stocking, refer to the embossing instructions, *page 71,* for the tree skirt, and emboss the 13×22" velvet rectangle with the small dragonfly rubber stamp.

For each stocking, use the stocking pattern to cut one piece from velvet, one from the backing, two from the lining fabric, and two from batting.

Sew the Stocking

The basic sewing steps are the same for all three stockings. After sewing the stocking and lining fronts and backs together, refer to the individual directions below for the cuffs and embellishments.

Machine-baste the batting shapes to the wrong side of the velvet stocking front and the stocking back. Sew the stocking front to the back, leaving the top edge open. Trim the seams, and clip the curves. Turn the stocking right side out. Finger-press the seams. Hand-sew the cording around the outside edges of the stocking.

Sew the stocking lining pieces together, leaving the top edge open. Trim the seam allowances, and clip curves; do not turn the lining right side out. Fold over ½" along the top edge of the lining to the wrong side; press.

Cuffed Stocking

Press under ¼" twice on each short edge of the 15×18" piece of sheer fabric. Fold the fabric in half to measure 7½×18". Slip-stitch the pressed edges together. Machine-baste the raw edges together.

Pin the cuff to the stocking, matching raw edges. The pressed edges of the cuff should touch the cording on the heel side of the stocking.

Baste the cuff to the stocking.

Turn under the raw edge at the top of the stocking; pin it in place. Slip the lining into the stocking with the wrong sides facing. Slip-stitch the lining to the stocking. Sew buttons on the cuff and stocking with silver and gold metallic threads.

For a hanging loop, fold the tieback in half, and make a square knot 2½" from the fold. Tack the knot to the top corner on the heel side of the stocking.

Dragonfly-Embossed Stocking

From the sheer gold fabric, cut an 11½×17½" rectangle for the cuff. Sew the short edges together, forming a circle. Fold the cuff in half with the wrong sides facing and the raw edges matching. Baste the raw edges together.

Cut the ⅛"-wide satin ribbon into twelve 18" lengths. Pin six of the ribbon lengths evenly around the outside of the cuff with the raw edges matching. Repeat on the inside of the cuff with the remaining ribbons. Slip the cuff onto the stocking, aligning the cuff seam with the heel seam and keeping the raw edges even. Machine-baste the cuff to the stocking, keeping the ribbons free. For the hanging loop, fold the ⅝"-wide sheer ribbon in half. Pin the loop to the top corner on the heel side of the stocking, aligning raw edges; sew.

Turn under the raw edge at the top of the stocking; pin it in place. Slip the lining into the stocking with the wrong sides facing. Slip-stitch the lining to the stocking.

Tie each pair of ribbons in a bow, creating poufs around the cuff. Fill each pouf with a small piece of fiberfill. Slip the corsage under a cuff bow; tack it in place. Use the tieback to make a bow around the corsage.

Leaf-Trimmed Stocking

For the hanging loop, fold a 9" length of ribbon in half. Pin the loop to the top corner on the heel side of the stocking, aligning the raw edges; sew. Turn under the raw edge at the top of the stocking; pin it in place. Slip the lining into the stocking with the wrong sides facing. Slip-stitch the lining to the stocking.

For the branch, cut an 18" length of copper wire, and 5" to 10" lengths of ribbon. Use narrow ribbons for the shorter lengths and wide ribbons for the longer lengths. Begin with the small leaves at the bottom of the branch, and work up the branch, increasing the size of the leaves. Cut a new length of wire as needed, and twist it around the end of the first wire.

To make the leaves, fold the ribbon lengths as shown in the diagram *below*. Neatly pinch together the ribbon ends, and turn in the ribbon at the sides. Tightly wrap wire around the folded ribbon. Thread a variety of beads on the wire. Make another leaf, and attach it to the branch next to the beads. Continue adding small, medium, and then large leaves to the branch until it

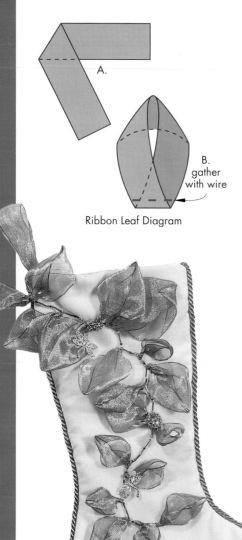

A.

B. gather with wire

Ribbon Leaf Diagram

reaches the desired length. Shape the branch on the stocking front, and tack it in place. Add dragonfly barrettes and buttons to the branch.

—*Designed by Laura Holtorf Collins*

NATURE'S LIGHT MANTELPIECE
Shown on page 66 and opposite.

YOU WILL NEED

Evergreen wall swag
6 assorted candleholders and candles
Gold tree branches
Oak leaf sprays
Floral spray paint: gold, silver, and copper
Large gold pinecones
Snowball ornaments
Snowflake ornaments
20-gauge copper soldering wire
Clear marbles

INSTRUCTIONS

Lay the swag on the mantel. Place the candleholders into and along the swag. Space the gold tree branches throughout the swag. (If gold branches are not available, spray natural branches with gold florist spray.) Spray-paint the oak leaves gold, silver, and copper. Insert the leaves into the arrangement. Add pinecones, snowball ornaments, and snowflake ornaments. Cut long lengths of copper wire; and referring to the Copper Wire Spirals instructions *(page 69)*, curl the wire and add marbles. Work the wire throughout the arrangement. Place candles in the candleholders.

—*Designed by Aubrey Dunbar*

NATIVITY WREATH
Shown on page 67.

YOU WILL NEED

Purchased wreath with pinecones
Gold tree branches
3 Golden Pinecone Tree Corsages
 (see page 69)
3 Teacup Arrangements (see page 70)
Ivy garland
Florist spray paint: gold, silver, and copper
20-gauge copper soldering wire
Scherenschnitte Nativity Ornaments

INSTRUCTIONS

Wire the gold branches to the wreath. (If gold branches are not available, spray natural branches with gold florist spray.) Attach the Golden Pinecone Tree Corsages to the wreath. Wire the Teacup Arrangements to the wreath. Spray paint the ivy leaves gold, silver, and copper. Fill in open areas on the wreath with ivy. Work several lengths of copper wire throughout the wreath. Curl the wire ends to hold the paper nativity ornaments.

—*Designed by Aubrey Dunbar*

SCHERENSCHNITTE NATIVITY
Shown on page 67.
The finished round ornaments are 5"
in diameter. Finished star ornament
is 7" wide.

YOU WILL NEED

Tracing paper and pencil
Lightweight white paper, such as typing paper
 or parchment
Transparent tape
Straight pin
Scherenschnitte, decoupage, or cuticle scissors

INSTRUCTIONS

Copy the desired pattern onto tracing paper. For the three-crowns pattern, place the traced pattern under a sheet of white paper. For the holy family, shepherd, and angel patterns, fold a sheet of white paper in half. Unfold the paper, and place the traced half-pattern under one-half of the white paper, aligning the pattern's dashed lines with the fold. For the star pattern, fold a sheet of white paper into fourths. Unfold the paper and placed the traced quarter-pattern under one-quarter of the white paper, aligning the pattern's dashed lines with the folds. Hold the papers together against a light box or sunny window, and trace the pattern onto the white paper with a sharp pencil. Remove the tracing paper pattern, and refold the white paper along the previous fold lines. Trim away the excess paper, leaving a 1" margin around the design. Tape the paper in several places to hold the layers together, being careful not to tape areas that you'll cut later.

Use a straight pin to poke a hole in the center of each white area shown on the pattern. Using the pinholes as starting points, cut out the smallest white area first, working with the scissors on the underside of the paper. Continue cutting out progressively larger areas, and then cut around the outside lines. For the holy family, unfold and trim away the beard from one of the figures as shown by the line for Mary's chin.

When all of the cutwork is done, carefully unfold the design and place it inside a book to flatten. Repeat to make additional ornaments.

—*Designed by Carole Behrer*

Place on fold

Scherenschnitte Nativity Patterns

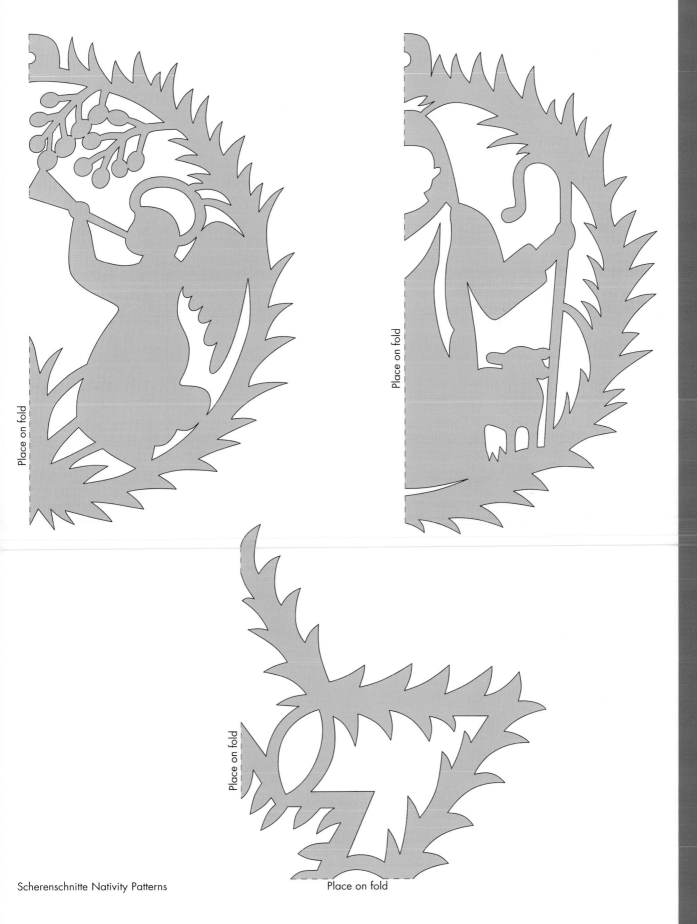

Scherenschnitte Nativity Patterns

Place on fold

Place on fold

Place on fold

Place on fold

LET IT
Snow!

When the weather outside is frightful, an indoor blizzard of

snowy designs looks purely delightful. Construct a snow

family from plastic-foam balls and dimensional paste (right)

for a centerpiece that's at home all winter long.

Instructions begin on page 84.

Easily add a painted snowman ornament to a basket, doorknob

or anything that needs a crafted wintery touch (above).

Four snow-people ornaments, each cut and painted to reflect its personality,

give this tree (opposite) a cold-weather theme. A star-shaped tree skirt tipped with

patchwork pines covers the table. Instructions begin on page 85.

Perched high on a snowdrift, a loving snowman stretches out his

arms in joy (above). Blanket stitching and buttons border the felt appliqué.

Fill a felt mitten (opposite) with winter greens or special treats.

Sewing is minimal—glue and fusible web do most of the work.

Instructions begin on page 91.

LET IT SNOW!

SNOW FAMILY

Shown on pages 78–79.
The snowmen range in height from
6½" to 11".

YOU WILL NEED

Plastic foam balls: 3"-, 4"-, and 5"-diameter
    for large snowman; 2½"-, 3"-, and
    4"-diameter for medium snowman; 2"-,
    2½"-, and 3"-diameter for small snowman
Beacon's Hold the Foam glue for plastic foam
11" bamboo skewers, one per snowman
Delta Decorative Snow paste or any dimensional
    paste, one to two jars per snowman
Twigs for the arms
Crafts glue
Paintbrushes: small round and an old,
    scruffy brush for the glue
Crystal glitter
Brown acrylic paint: burnt umber
1¼×18" strip of heather gray fleece for
    the scarf
Cream fleece: 1¾×14" strip for the scarf and
    2¾"-diameter circle for the hat
⅝"-diameter rhinestone button
Small cream pom-pom
Seed pearls

INSTRUCTIONS

Cut off one side of the largest ball for
each snowman, making a flat surface
for it to stand. Apply a dab of the
foam glue between adjacent balls. Push
a skewer through the center to hold

Photo 1

the balls in place while the
glue dries. The skewer also
serves as a handle when the
paste is applied.

When the glue is dry, use
Decorative Snow paste to coat the
snowman forms, except for the flat
bottom surfaces. While the paste is still
wet, push twigs into opposite sides of
each center ball for arms. For each
nose, break off approximately ¾" to 1"
from the end of a skewer and insert it
into the face. Dab a small amount of
paste onto the twig arms; let the paste
dry for a minimum of 24 hours or
until completely firm.

Photo 2

Break off the skewer even with the
top of each head. Brush the top ⅓ to ½
of each ball with crafts glue, taking
care to generously cover the ends of

skewers. Set the snowmen on clean
paper to save the excess glitter. Shake
crystal glitter over the wet glue; let the
glitter and glue set.

Paint the noses and eyes brown
with a small round brush; let the
paint dry.

Fringe the narrow edges of the gray
fleece strip, making 1½"-long cuts
spaced ¼" apart. Tie the gray scarf
around the large snowman's neck with
an overhand knot.

Fringe the narrow edges of the
cream fleece strip, making 1"-long cuts
spaced ¼" apart. Wrap the cream scarf
around the medium snowman's neck,
and sew the button through both
layers to secure it. To make the cap,
hand-sew gathering stitches ⅛" from
the edges of the fleece circle. Pull the
thread until the cap measures
approximately 2" across; knot the
thread. Sew a cream pom-pom to the
top of the cap. Sew pearls randomly
over the top of the cap. Glue the cap
to the medium snowman's head.

—Designed by Beverly Rivers

SNOW FAMILY PICKET FENCE

Shown on pages 78–79.
The picket fence is 4¼×18×9".

YOU WILL NEED

- Scrollsaw and #5R blade
- Scrap of ⅜" pine or Baltic birch plywood
- ⅛" Baltic birch plywood
- 1/16" Baltic birch plywood
- Woodworker's glue
- White acrylic paint
- #12 flat synthetic paintbrush
- Miniature evergreen and ball garlands
- 4 — 1½"-diameter wreaths

INSTRUCTIONS

From the ½" pine, cut four ⅜×⅜×4¼" pieces for the corner posts; round off one end for the top of corner post. From the ⅛" Baltic birch plywood, cut four ⅛×⅜×18" pieces and four ⅛×⅜×9" pieces for the rails. From the 1/16" Baltic birch plywood, cut thirty-two 1/16×¼×4¼" pieces for the pickets. Cut one end of each picket into a point.

Use a pencil to make marks 1½" apart on one side of each 18" rail. Lay two rails 1½" apart, marked side up, on a flat surface. Glue the pickets centered over the marks on the rails with the bottom of each picket 1⅛" below the bottom rail. Glue a corner post even with the ends of the rails. Repeat for the remaining two 18" rails. Also repeat for the four 9" rails, eliminating the corner posts. When the glue is dry, stand the fence sections, and glue the ends of the 9" rails to the corner posts. Let the glue dry.

Paint the picket fence white; let the paint dry. Drape the evergreen garland then the ball garland over the pickets. Add a wreath to each corner post.

—Designed by Beverly Rivers

OUT-ON-A-LIMB SNOWMAN ORNAMENT

Shown on pages 78 and 80.
The ornament is 5" tall.

YOU WILL NEED

- FolkArt Colors: Buttercrunch 737 (BC), Licorice 938 (LI), Maroon 415 (MA), and Taffy 902 (TA)
- #12 synthetic flat brush
- #2 synthetic liner brush
- ⅛×2×3½" Baltic birch plywood
- Drill and drill bit
- ⅛×1" dowel
- Scrollsaw and #5R blade
- Tracing and transfer paper
- 100- and 150-grit sandpaper
- Tack cloth
- Wood sealer
- 5-minute epoxy
- Antiquing medium
- Small tree branch
- 12" of 18-gauge wire

INSTRUCTIONS

Duplicate the snowman and the star patterns with tracing paper. Copy the outlines onto a 2×3×½" piece of ⅛" Baltic birch plywood with transfer paper. Cut out the pieces with a scrollsaw, using a #5R blade.

Drill a ⅛" hole for the snowman's nose where shown on the pattern, and a hanging hole on the star. Sand or sharpen one end of a ⅛" dowel to a point, then cut off ¼" from the pointed end for the nose.

Sand all surfaces with 100- and then 150-grit sandpaper. Remove sanding dust with a tack cloth. Apply wood sealer to all surfaces, and allow the sealer to dry. Then sand again with 150-grit sandpaper, and wipe clean with a tack cloth.

Base-coat all surfaces of the snowman TA, the star BC, and the heart MA. Allow the paint to dry; lightly sand with 150-grit sandpaper.

Attach the nose to the snowman with 5-minute epoxy, and allow the epoxy to set. Dip the end of a stylus or toothpick into LI, and dot the snowman's eyes and mouth. Let the dots dry. (Because of the thickness, dots take longer to dry.) Antique the pieces with antiquing medium.

Using a #2 liner brush, apply the stitching lines to the snowman, the star, and the heart.

To suspend the snowman from the branch, sand off a spot on the back of the snowman, and attach a wire end with epoxy. Twist the wire around the branch several times. Allow 1" hanging distance, and thread the wire through the star. Twist a loop and secure by wrapping the wire, then cut the excess wire with scissors or wire cutters.

—Designed by Pat Harmon

1/16" hole

1/8" hole
1/16" deep

Out-On-A-Limb
Snowman Ornament Pattern

PICKET-FENCE SNOWMEN ORNAMENT

Shown on pages 78, 80, and above.

YOU WILL NEED

¼×2×13" pine
⅛×⅜×7" Baltic birch plywood
Scrollsaw and #5R blade
100- and 150-grit sandpaper
Tack cloth
Transfer and tracing paper
FolkArt Colors: Barnyard Red 611 (BD),
    Licorice 938 (LI), Paprika 744 (PP), and
    Wicker White 901 (WW)
Paintbrushes: #6 synthetic flat, #00 synthetic
    liner, and spatter brush or old toothbrush
5-minute epoxy
Antiquing medium
Satin-finish varnish
Scraps of assorted fabrics
5-minute epoxy
5" length of 19-gauge wire
12" length of jute

INSTRUCTIONS

Duplicate the snowmen patterns with tracing paper. Copy the body outlines onto ¼" pine. Drill ¹⁄₁₆" holes where shown on the pattern. Cut out the shapes with a scrollsaw. For the hat brims, cut three ¼×1½" pieces of ⅛" Baltic birch plywood.

Sand all surfaces with 100- and then 150-grit sandpaper. Apply wood sealer to all surfaces, and allow the sealer to dry.

Base-coat large areas with a #6 flat brush, and apply details with a #00 liner brush. Base-coat the mother's hat front BD, and paint the remaining two hat fronts LI. Paint all remaining areas of the snowmen WW. Paint one hat brim BD and the other two LI. Let the paint dry.

Copy the face details onto the cutouts, or paint them freehand. Dip a cotton swab into BD, then wipe off most of the paint on a paper towel. Lightly blush all cheeks.

Dip the large end of a stylus into LI, and dot all eyes and mouths. Dot the mother's nose LI. Paint all remaining noses PP.

Thin WW with water to ink consistency. With a spatter brush or an old toothbrush, spatter (flyspeck) the ornaments. Using 100-grit sandpaper, sand the edges of all cutouts. Sand paint off a spot on the front and back of each cutout where the pieces join. Epoxy the two small snowmen to the large snowman, and all brims to the hats. Let the epoxy set.

Antique all surfaces with your favorite antiquing medium, let the medium dry thoroughly, and then spray with satin-finish varnish. Tear fabric into ½"-wide strips, wrap the strips around the snowmen's necks, and trim them to size. Thread 19-gauge wire through the ornament holes, and twist the ends to secure. Cut two 6" lengths of jute, put the pieces together, and tie them in a bow around the wire hanger.

—Designed by Debbie Currin

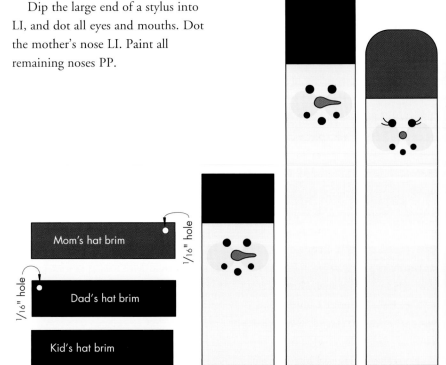

Picket-Fence Ornament Pattern

CRACKLED SNOWMAN ORNAMENT
Shown on page 80 and right.

YOU WILL NEED

Tracing and transfer paper
$\frac{1}{2} \times 2 \times 4$" pine
$\frac{1}{8} \times 1 \times 1$" Baltic birch plywood
$\frac{3}{8}$" length of $\frac{1}{4}$" dowel
$\frac{3}{4}$" length of $\frac{1}{8}$" dowel
#217 $\frac{1}{2}$" screw eye
Scrollsaw and #5R blade
Drill and drill bits
100- and 150-grit sandpaper
Tack cloth
5-minute epoxy
Delta Ceramcoat Colors: Black 2506 (BK), Fire Red 2083 (FR). Georgia Clay 2097 (GC), Light Ivory 2401 (LI), and Midnight 2114 (MI)
#12 synthetic flat
#6 synthetic round
DecoArt Weathered-Wood crackle medium
Satin-finish spray varnish
Antiquing medium
2 — $1\frac{1}{2}$"-long twigs, each approximately $\frac{1}{8}$" in diameter
$\frac{3}{8} \times 7$" plaid wool fabric scrap
Black thread

INSTRUCTIONS

Trace the patterns and transfer the body onto a $\frac{1}{2} \times 2 \times 4$" piece of pine. Transfer the hat-brim circle onto the $\frac{1}{8} \times 1 \times 1$" plywood, and drill the $\frac{1}{4}$" hole where shown. Cut out the pieces with a scrollsaw, using a #5R blade. Drill $\frac{1}{8}$" and $\frac{1}{32}$" holes where shown on the pattern. Sand all surfaces in the direction of the grain with 100- and then 150-grit sandpaper. Round one end of the $\frac{1}{8}$"-diameter nose dowel with 100-grit sandpaper. Remove the sanding dust with a tack cloth.

Epoxy the $\frac{1}{4}$" dowel into the hat-brim circle, and let the epoxy set.

Attach the screw eye to the hat, and paint it when you paint the hat.

Base-coat the front, back, and edges of the hat BK. Paint the nose dowel GC. Base-coat the front, back, and edges of the snowman MI, and let the paint dry thoroughly. Then apply a generous coat of crackle medium over the MI. Let the crackle medium dry for a minimum of one hour.

Brush one coat of LI over the crackle medium. Allow the LI to dry completely. To protect the crackled finish, lightly mist all surfaces with two coats of spray varnish. Next, dip a stylus or the handle end of a small brush into BK. Dot the snowman's mouth and eyes. With the round brush, paint BK round or GC heart shaped buttons.

Antique all surfaces with your favorite antiquing medium, and allow the medium to dry thoroughly.

Dip the ends of the nose dowel and the arm twigs into epoxy. Insert the nose and arms into the drilled holes, and allow the epoxy to set. Sand paint from the top of the snowman's head, and epoxy the hat to the head. (Glue and epoxy won't bond permanently to painted or varnished surfaces.)

For a fringed scarf, fray the ends of the fabric strip by pulling the loose threads. Tie the scarf around the snowman's neck. Apply a dot of epoxy to the back of the scarf knot to secure the scarf to the snowman. To hang, thread black thread through the screw eye and knot the ends to secure.

—*Designed by Peggy Kahler*

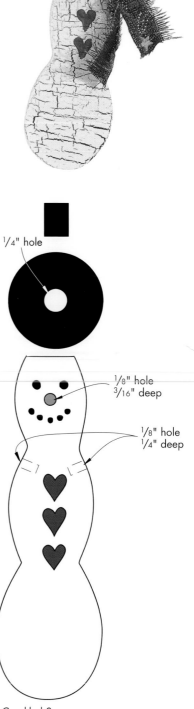

$\frac{1}{4}$" hole

$\frac{1}{8}$" hole
$\frac{3}{16}$" deep

$\frac{1}{8}$" hole
$\frac{1}{4}$" deep

Crackled Snowman
Ornament Pattern

SNOWMAN-IN-A-BOX ORNAMENT

Shown on page 80 and above.

YOU WILL NEED

2¼×1×2" wooden box
Drill and drill bit
2⅜" person game piece
Paintbrushes: flat, round, and liner
Delta Ceramcoat Colors Acrylic paint:
 Bittersweet Orange 2041 (BO), Black 2506
 (BK), Burgundy Rose 2123 (BU), and
 Magnolia White 2487 (MA)
10" length of 20-gauge wire
Block of floral foam
½×6" strip of fabric
Greenery, berries, cinnamon sticks,
 and cinnamon heart
Glue gun and hotmelt adhesive
Delta Decorative Snow
Satin-finish spray varnish

INSTRUCTIONS

Drill a small hanging hole in each side of the box. Using the flat brush, paint the box BU and the game piece MA; let the paint dry. With the liner brush, paint the snowman's nose BO and his mouth BK. Using the handle end of the brush, dot the eyes BK. Scrub the cheeks BU with the round brush.

Wind the wire around a pencil to form a spiral shape. Remove the pencil, and pull the wire ends to get the desired shape. Insert the wire ends through the drilled holes, and trim the ends. Trim the blocks of floral foam to fit inside the bottom half of the box. Tie the fabric strip around the snowman's neck for a scarf. Glue the cinnamon heart to the box. Arrange the snowman, greenery, berries, and cinnamon sticks by inserting the ends into the foam block and securing them with glue if necessary. Liberally apply the snow texture medium to the top edges of the box and cinnamon sticks; let the medium dry. Spray the finished ornament with satin-finish varnish.

—*Designed by Pat Olson and Kristin Olson Johnson*

STAR-TIPS TREE SKIRT

Shown on page 80.
The finished skirt is 44" in diameter.

YOU WILL NEED

Quilting template material
1 yard of red print fabric
¼ yard of green print fabric
⅓ yard of ivory print fabric
Scraps of brown print fabric
1½ yards fabric for back
1½ yards quilt batting
Sewing thread
Graph paper
8—1"-diameter red buttons
Large hook-and-eye fastener

INSTRUCTIONS

All pieces include a ¼" seam allowance. Press seams toward the darker fabric.

Enlarge the patterns, cut out, and transfer to template material.

From the red print, cut eight of Pattern A and enough 1½"-wide strips to equal 6 yards (216"). From the ivory print, cut eight of Pattern B, eight of Pattern B reversed, eight of Pattern C, and eight of Pattern C reversed. From the green print, cut eight of the tree pattern. From the brown print, cut eight of the tree-trunk pattern.

For each panel, referring to Diagram 1, sew a B piece to each side of the tree piece. Sew a C piece to each side of the tree-trunk piece. Sew the tree-trunk unit to the tree unit. Sew the completed tree unit to an A piece. Repeat to make a total of eight panels.

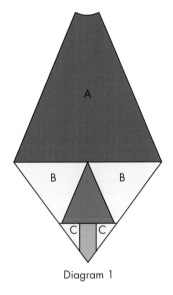

Diagram 1

Referring to Diagram 2, sew the edges of the C pieces together in a circle, leaving one seam unstitched for the opening. Layer the back, the batting, and the pieced top; baste.

Quilt ¼" from the seam line on the straight edges of the C piece. Quilt ⅛" outside the seams of the trees and trunks. Trim the backing and batting even with the edges of the top.

Sew the short ends of the 1½"-wide strips together using diagonal seams to make one continuous piece. Trim seams to ¼". Press under ¼" on one long edge. Sew the unpressed edge to the back side of the quilted skirt, right sides together, folding a tuck into each inner point and mitering each outer point. Turn the binding over the raw edge and sew to the front of the skirt. Sew a button in the center of each tree. Sew a large hook-and-eye fastener to the top edges of the opening

—*Designed by Phyllis Dobbs*

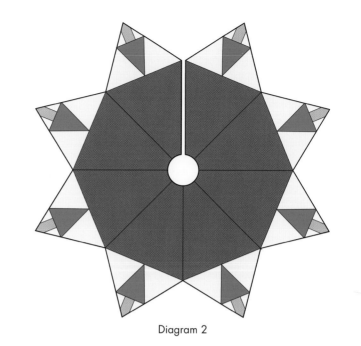

Diagram 2

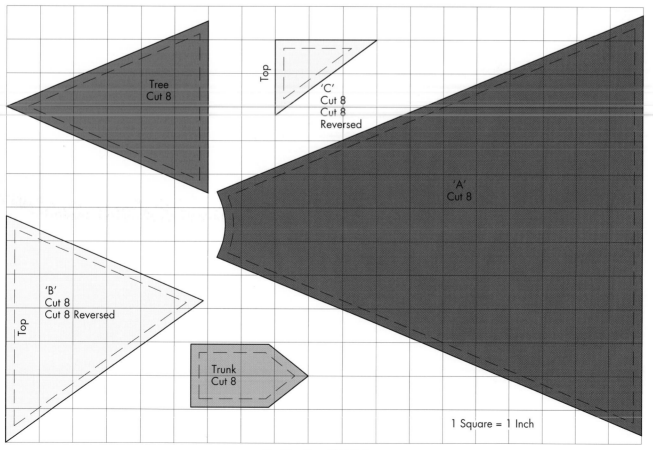

Star-Tips Tree Skirt Patterns

RED-COAT SNOWMAN ORNAMENT
Shown on page 81.

YOU WILL NEED

Tracing and transfer paper
1/8×6×4" Baltic birch plywood
Scrollsaw and #5R blade
Drill and 1/16" drill bit
100- and 150-grit sandpaper
Tack cloth
Wood sealer
DecoArt Americana Acrylic Colors:
  Buttermilk DA3 (BU), Cranberry Wine
  DA112 (CW), Georgia Clay DA17 (GC),
  Honey Brown DA163 (HB), Khaki Tan
  DA173 (KT), Lamp Black DA67 (LB), and
  Light Cinnamon DA114 (LC)
Paintbrushes: #8 synthetic flat, #10/0
  synthetic liner, and splatter brush or
  old toothbrush
Antiquing medium
2—3/8"-diameter red buttons
12" of twine
Crafts glue

INSTRUCTIONS

Transfer the outline of the ornament from the pattern onto 1/8" Baltic birch plywood. Cut out the shape with a scrollsaw, using a #5R blade. Drill a hole at the top of the head where shown on the pattern. Sand all surfaces with 100- and then 150-grit sandpaper. Remove the sanding dust with a tack cloth.

Apply wood sealer to all surfaces and let it dry. Sand again with 150-grit sandpaper, and wipe with a tack cloth.

Transfer the main pattern lines to the ornament. There's no need to copy the details yet—you'll base-coat over them. Lightly sand with a paper

grocery sack to remove fuzz raised by acrylic paint; remove the sanding dust with a tack cloth.

With the #8 flat brush, base-coat the head and body BU, the jacket CW, and the mittens HB. Let the paint dry. Then lightly brush CW on the cheeks, paint the nose GC, and dot the eyes and mouth LB. Shade the jacket with CW and LB mixed 4:1; dilute the mixture with water to ink consistency, and use a liner brush to paint the lines on the jacket. Float KT shading on the snowman and LC shading on the mittens.

Apply antiquing medium to the ornament. Let the medium dry. Dilute LB with water to ink consistency. Dip a spatter brush or an old toothbrush into the paint; spatter (flyspeck) the cutout. Thread a 6" length of twine through the hole in the ornament, and knot the ends. Cut the remaining twine in two pieces. Thread each piece through the holes in a button and knot close to the button. Trim the ends short. Glue the buttons to the snowman's coat.

—*Designed by Myra Mahy*

1/16" hole

Red-Coat Snowman Ornament Pattern

HEART-FELT SNOWMAN TABLE RUNNER
Shown on page 82.

YOU WILL NEED

1/2 yard of 72"-wide cranberry felt
1/2 yard of 72"-wide taupe felt
1/2 yard of 72"-wide white felt
9×12" piece of black felt
9×12" piece of hunter green felt
Graph paper
1 yard of paper-backed fusible adhesive
#3 perle cotton: cranberry, white, black, hunter
  green, and orange
About 45 white pearl buttons in assorted colors

INSTRUCTIONS

From the cranberry felt, cut a 16½×27" rectangle, two 2×25" strips, and two 2×16½" strips. Set the remaining felt aside. From the taupe felt, cut a 16½×27" rectangle.

Enlarge the patterns, *page 92;* cut out. Turn each pattern wrong side up on the paper side of the fusible adhesive and trace around it; cut out. Referring to the photograph on *page 82,* arrange the scarf and heart pieces on the cranberry felt; snowman and snow mounds on the white felt; the tree trunks, arms, and hat on the black felt; and the trees on green felt. Fuse according to manufacturer's directions. Cut out the pieces and remove the paper backing. Arrange the pieces on the taupe rectangle and fuse. Use corresponding colors of #3 perle cotton to blanket-stitch around each piece. Add black French-knot eyes and mouth to the snowman. Use orange perle cotton and straight stitches to stitch a carrot nose.

Center the 2×25" strips across the top and bottom edges of the taupe rectangle. Use black perle cotton to work blanket stitches through all layers along the inside 25" edge of each strip. Center the 2×16½" strips across the sides, covering the ends of the longer strips. Work blanket stitches through all layers along the inside 16½" edge of each strip.

Center the taupe rectangle atop the cranberry rectangle, aligning edges. Use black perle cotton to work blanket stitches all the way around the outer edge. Arrange the buttons on the cranberry strips. To tie them in place, thread a needle with black perle cotton. Insert the needle from the front, through one hole in the button, holding the tail so it doesn't pull

through. Return the needle to the front through the other button hole. Tie the perle cotton in a square knot and trim the ends about ¼" beyond the knot.

—Designed by Sandy Belt

MITTEN DOOR HANGER
Shown on page 83.
The mitten is 20" tall.

YOU WILL NEED

Graph paper
Felt: ½ yard of burgundy and a scrap of heather gray
12" square of Warm & Natural cotton batting
Fabric: a 2¼×18" torn strip of flannel for the scarf, a 1¼×6" torn strip of flannel for the hanging loop, and assorted scraps for the stars
Paper-backed fusible webbing
Brown perle cotton
Embroidery needle
Pebbles: four for the buttons and two for the eyes
Black acrylic paint
Paintbrush
Purchased miniature carrot
8"-long ⅛"-diameter twig
1½×3" piece of rusted tin
6" length of jute
Package of ¼" white pom-poms
Crafts glue

INSTRUCTIONS

Enlarge patterns, *page 93;* and cut out. From burgundy felt, cut two mittens. From cotton batting, cut one snowman body and one of each arm. From heather-gray felt, cut one bucket.

Turn the star patterns upside down and trace around them on the paper side of the fusible webbing; cut out. Fuse the webbing pieces to the assorted fabric scraps, following the

manufacturer's instructions. Cut out the stars. Remove the paper backings.

Referring to the photo on *page 83,* place the snowman's body on the front mitten. For the scarf, wrap the 2¼×18" flannel strip around the snowman's neck. Pin the snowman in position, and pin the arms in place. To sew the body and arms to the mitten, make random straight stitches with brown perle cotton. Position the stars on the mitten; fuse them in place. Use brown perle cotton to stem-stitch vertical lines at the top of the mitten for cuff.

Pin together the mitten front and back. Make irregular straight stitches with perle cotton to sew the mittens together, leaving the top edge open. Fold the 1¼×6" flannel strip in half, and glue the ends to the inside left corner for a hanging loop.

Paint the pebbles black for the eyes and buttons; let the paint dry. Glue the eyes, carrot nose, and buttons in place. For the shovel, glue the twig in the snowman's arms; curve the tin, and glue it to the end of the twig handle. Glue the arms in position. Crumple the scarf around the neck, and drape it over the body; glue it in place. Poke a hole in each top corner of the bucket. Stick one end of the jute through each hole; tie an overhand knot in each end. Glue the bucket in place, leaving the top open. For snowballs, glue pom-poms in the bucket and at the bottom right corner.

—Designed by Sandy Dye

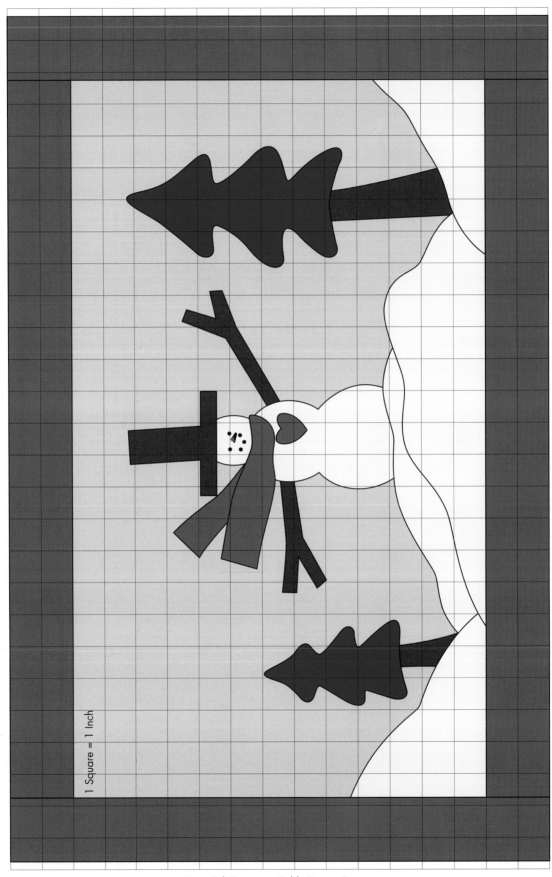

1 Square = 1 Inch

Heart-Felt Snowman Table Runner Pattern

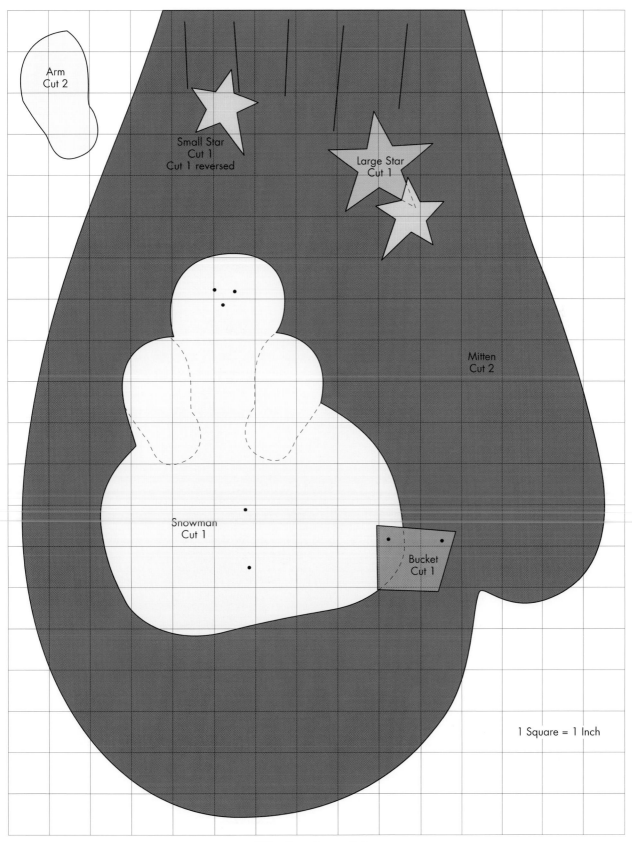

Arm
Cut 2

Small Star
Cut 1
Cut 1 reversed

Large Star
Cut 1

Mitten
Cut 2

Snowman
Cut 1

Bucket
Cut 1

1 Square = 1 Inch

Mitten Door Hanger Pattern

A Christmas Kitchen

Old favorites lend a warm feeling to holiday gifts and decorating. A gleaming silver garland, shiny embossed boxes, fabric-topped jars packed with homemade goodies, and vintage spoons painted with jolly Santas are gifts from your kitchen and heart that will be enjoyed long past the holidays. Instructions begin on page 102.

*A trio of soft-sculpture topiaries (opposite) is reminiscent of
Provence with painted European-style pots and French-inspired fabrics.
The wooden bowl (above) is dressed for success with a strand of beads.
Paint the beads and sand them for an aged look, then secure
them to the bowl with twine and screw eyes.
Instructions begin on page 104.*

Blocky candleholders (above) have the look of old architecture even

though they're made of new molding from the lumberyard.

Dish up some fun with a kitchen tree (opposite). Use acrylics to paint

Santa faces on vintage spoons, then tie them to a tiny pine.

Instructions begin on page 105.

*Give drink and baking mixes, layered into jars and
tied with country trims (opposite). Each mix makes treats that
are sure to be appreciated on long winter nights.
Wooden spools from the crafts store and half circles of plywood shape
a 15-inch-tall shelf (below) that's reminiscent of tramp art.
Recipes and project instructions begin on page 106.*

Silver leaf, metallic paint, and rubbing cream lend a mellow look to these quick crafts. Paint precut letters silver, cover them with silver foil, and string on a chain for a great holiday swag. Papier-mâché boxes with embossed designs take on the look of old tin ceiling tiles when you rub them with silver buffing cream. Instructions begin at right.

FAUX-TIN GIFT BOXES
Shown above and on pages 94 and 101.

YOU WILL NEED
Papier-mâché boxes
White acrylic paint
Sponge brush
Silver Rub 'n Buff
Green tissue paper
1"-wide green ribbon
Quick Candies
Green raffia
Small cookie cutters
Sprigs of white berries

INSTRUCTIONS
Use the sponge brush to base-coat the papier-mâché boxes white; allow the paint to dry. Apply silver Rub'n Buff to the outside surfaces of the lids and to the sides of the bases. When the boxes are dry, line them with tissue paper and fill them with candies. Place the lids on the boxes. Wrap a ribbon around the boxes, securing a cookie cutter with the ribbon. Tie bows with the ribbon, securing the berry springs. Use raffia to tie a second bow around each bow.

—*Designed by Eric Powers*

QUICK CANDIES
Shown at right.

YOU WILL NEED
Wilton White Candy Melts
Wilton Microwavable Squeeze Bottle
Wilton Icing Color: Juniper Green
Candy molds

INSTRUCTIONS
Place the candies in the bottle and melt in a microwave following the manufacturer's instructions. Add a small amount of coloring, if you desire, and stir. Fill the molds with the melted candy. Tap the mold lightly to eliminate air bubbles. Smooth the edges with a knife if necessary. Let the candies cool in the refrigerator; invert the molds to release the formed candies.

—*Designed by Eric Powers*

TOPIARY TREES

Shown on page 96.
The topiaries are 14" to 18" tall.

YOU WILL NEED

Clay flowerpot or wooden container, approximately 4½" tall

Plaid FolkArt Acrylic colors: French Vanilla 431 (FV) and Hauser Green 460 (HG)

Paintbrushes: 1" sponge

Florist's foam

¼ yard cotton print fabric

Needle and sewing thread

Polyester fiberfill

10" to 14" length of ⅜"-diameter tree branch

Glue gun and hotmelt adhesive

Variety of decorations, such as torn fabric strips, twine, raffia, ribbon, small nest with eggs, and cinnamon sticks

Deer moss

INSTRUCTIONS

Base-coat the flowerpot or container HG. Before the base coat dries, apply a light coat of FV with a dry brush using a slip-slap method. This will allow some of the base coat to show through. Let the paint dry, then lightly dry-brush FV over the green.

Fill the pot or container with florist's foam and glue in place.

The trees can be made with circles, triangles, or a combination of both. For the large triangular tree section, cut three 7¼"-tall triangles with 5½" bases and one triangle with equal 5½" sides. For the small triangular tree section, cut three 5½"-tall triangles with 5" bases and one triangle with equal 5" sides. For the round tree sections, cut pairs of 6"-, 5½"-, or 5"-diameter circles. All the bottom round sections on our trees are made with 6"-diameter circles.

Sew all pieces with right sides together using ¼"-seam allowances. To make the triangular tree sections, sew together the long edges of the three large triangles, beginning and ending ¼" from the ends. Cut a ½"-slit in the center of the small triangle to insert the branch. Sew the small triangle to the short edges of the large triangles, leaving an opening for turning. Turn right side out and stuff with polyester fiberfill. Slip-stitch the opening closed.

To make the round tree sections, sew together two circles, leaving a ½"- and a 1½"-opening opposite each other on the circle. If the round section is for the top of the topiary, leave only a 1½"-opening. Turn right side out through the 1½"-opening and stuff with fiberfill.

To create the trees, insert the branch through the openings in the round sections and the slits in the

bottom of the triangular sections. Add more fiberfill if needed. Sew the openings closed to fit tightly around the branch. Insert the bottom of the branch in the center of the florist's foam; glue in place.

Glue moss around the base of the tree to cover the florist's foam. Referring to the photo, decorate the tree by making bows of torn fabric strips, or by tying a bow around the branch trunk with ribbon, twine, raffia, or torn fabric strips. Finally, glue a nest with eggs or a bundle of cinnamon sticks at the base of the tree.

—Designed by Martha Sutyak

LET-IT-BEAD BOWL

Shown on page 97.
The bowl is 11" in diameter and 6" tall.

YOU WILL NEED

Wooden bowl

105—½"-diameter white barrel-shape beads

7—³⁄₁₆" screw eyes

Delta Ceramcoat Colors: Dark Forest 2096 (DF), Green Sea 2445 (GS), and Light Ivory 2401 (LI)

Small flat synthetic brush and 2" sponge

150-grit sandpaper

Jute

Spray-matte varnish

INSTRUCTIONS

***Note:** You may need to adjust the bead spacing to fit your bowl.*

With a sponge brush, paint all surfaces of the bowl LI using a slip-slap motion. Apply two coats of paint, allowing ample drying time between coats.

Lightly sand 35 beads to remove the finish. With the flat brush, paint 20 beads GS. Paint the remaining sanded beads DF. Lightly sand some beads for a worn finish.

Twist the screw eyes into the top of the bowl at seven evenly spaced intervals. Tie the end of a 36"-long string onto a screw eye, and thread the string with 15 beads. Thread the string through the next screw eye, and continue to thread it with beads around the bowl. When you have strung beads through all screw eyes, tie the string ends together, and trim the ends. Apply a coat of varnish, and let the varnish dry.

—*Designed by Martha Sutyak*

PINE-MOLDING CANDLEHOLDERS

Shown on page 98.
The candleholders are 6" and 9" tall.

YOU WILL NEED

84×3" fluted pine molding
½×3½×9" Baltic birch plywood
Scrollsaw, saber saw, or band saw
3 — 3" tin stars
Hammer and brads
Paintbrush: 2" sponge brush
Delta Ceramcoat Colors: Light Ivory 2401 (LI)
Satin-finish varnish

INSTRUCTIONS

Cut eight pieces of molding 6" long, and four pieces 9" long. Cut the plywood into three 3½×3" pieces. Assemble the candleholders by securing the molding pieces with brads where each side overlaps the front and back molding pieces. Nail the plywood tops in place.

Paint the candleholders with two coats of LI; let the paint dry. Apply a coat of varnish; and let dry completely. Attach the stars with brads.

—*Designed by Martha Sutyak*

SPOONFUL-OF-SANTA ORNAMENTS

Shown on pages 94, 95, 99, and below.

YOU WILL NEED

Old silver spoons
Transfer and tracing paper
Delta Perm Enamel Colors; Metal Primer, Country Tomato 017 (CT), Light Peach 011 (LP), Mushroom 018 (MU), Ultra Black 034 (UB), Ultra White 029 (UW), and Satin Glaze
Paintbrushes: Flat, round, and liner and a spatter brush or old toothbrush
Ribbon or raffia for ties

INSTRUCTIONS

Thoroughly clean the spoons. With the flat brush apply the metal primer, following the manufacturer's instructions. Then base-coat the bowl of each spoon MU. Copy the pattern onto tracing paper, and transfer it onto the spoons using transfer paper. Copy only the outlines of the designs. There's no need to copy the details yet—you'll base-coat over them.

Using the flat brush, base-coat Santa's coat and hat CT, his face LP, and his beard, mustache, and hat trim UW. Apply MU shading around Santa's beard with the flat brush. With a liner brush, paint his bangs UW and his mouth UB. Using the handle end of the brush, dot the eyes UB. Scrub his cheeks CT with the round brush. Use UW and the spatter brush to spatter (flyspeck) snow on the spoons. Apply the satin glaze and let it dry.

—*Designed by Pat Olson*

Spoonful-of-Santa
Ornament Pattern

VIENNESE COFFEE-BALL MIX
Shown on page 100 and below.

YOU WILL NEED

2 cups shortbread cookie crumbs or packaged
   chocolate chip cookies, crushed
   (about ¾ of a 10-ounce package)
1¼ to 1½ cups sifted powdered sugar
2 tablespoons unsweetened cocoa powder
1½ teaspoons instant coffee crystals or instant
   espresso powder
¾ teaspoon ground cinnamon
1 cup chopped nuts, lightly toasted and cooled

INSTRUCTIONS

Layer ingredients in a 1-quart canning jar or decorative canister. Gently tap the jar on the counter to settle each layer before adding the next one. Add additional nuts to fill small gaps in the jar, if necessary. Makes 1 jar.

Preparation Instructions

Place jar contents in a large mixing bowl. Add 4 to 5 tablespoons espresso, strong coffee, or water, using just enough to moisten. Form into 1¼-inch balls; roll generously in ½ cup sifted powdered sugar. Place on a sheet of waxed paper and let stand until dry (about 1 hour). Before serving, roll again in powdered sugar, if desired. Store in an airtight container for up to 1 week. Makes about 30.

CHAI MIX
Shown on page 100.

YOU WILL NEED

1¼ cups nonfat dry milk powder
¼ cup black tea leaves
12 cardamom pods
4 — 2-inch pieces cinnamon stick
2 teaspoons dried lemon peel

INSTRUCTIONS

Place all ingredients in a 12-ounce jar or bottle. Makes 1 jar.

Preparation Instructions

Place jar contents in large saucepan with 8 cups of water. Bring to boil. Remove the saucepan from the heat, cover, and let set for 5 minutes. Strain through a wire strainer lined with cheesecloth or coffee filter. Serve, sweetening with honey to taste. Makes 8 (1-cup) servings.

CHRISTMAS BISCOTTI MIX
Shown on pages 94 and 100.

YOU WILL NEED

¾ cup dried cranberries or dried cherries
¾ cup chopped shelled green pistachios
2 cups all-purpose flour
½ teaspoon ground cardamom
2 teaspoons baking powder
⅔ cup Vanilla Sugar

INSTRUCTIONS

Combine the cranberries and pistachios. Layer the alternately with remaining ingredients in two 1-pint canning jars. Gently tap jar on the counter to settle each layer before adding the next one. Add additional dried fruits or pistachios to fill small gaps, if necessary. Makes 2 jars.

Vanilla Sugar: Fill a quart jar with 4 cups sugar. Cut a vanilla bean in half lengthwise and insert both halves into sugar. Secure lid and store in a cool, dry place for several weeks before using. Keeps indefinitely.

Preparation Instructions

Beat 3 tablespoons butter (no substitutes) in a large mixing bowl with an electric mixer on medium speed for 30 seconds. Beat in 1 egg. Stir in jar contents until combined, using a wooden spoon. Cover and chill until easy to handle, if necessary.

Shape the dough into a 9-inch loaf. Place on a lightly greased cookie sheet, flattening slightly to 2 inches wide.

Bake in a 375° oven for 25 to 30 minutes or until a wooden toothpick inserted near the center comes out clean. Cool on the cookie sheet for 1 hour. Diagonally cut the loaf into ½"-thick slices using a serrated knife. Place slices, cut side down, on ungreased cookie sheet(s).

Bake in a 325° oven for 8 minutes. Turn over slices; bake 8 to 10 minutes more or until dry and crisp. Transfer to a wire rack to cool. Makes 16.

CAFE AU LAIT MIX

Shown on pages 94 and 100.

YOU WILL NEED

½ cup powdered nondairy creamer
½ cup buttermints, lightly crushed
¼ cup sifted powdered sugar
2 cups nonfat dry milk powder
⅔ cup instant coffee crystals
Peppermint sticks or round hard candies

INSTRUCTIONS

Stir together nondairy creamer, buttermints, powdered sugar, and milk powder. Layer with coffee crystals. Insert candies to snugly fill jars. Makes 1 quart.

Preparation Instructions

For each serving, place ¼ cup of mix in a mug, and add ⅔ cup boiling water. Stir until mix dissolves. Serve with a peppermint stick or candy, if you desire.

GOOD NIGHT SANTA COCOA MIX

Shown on page 94 and 100.

See cocoa recipe on *page 36.*

MINIATURE SPOOL SHELF

Shown on pages 101.

YOU WILL NEED

3/16×14×20" Baltic birch plywood
Scrollsaw
21—2" unfinished spools
100- and 150-grit sandpaper
5-minute epoxy
1" flat brush
Plaid FolkArt acrylic paint:
    French Vanilla 431 (FV)
Matte-finish varnish

INSTRUCTIONS

Trace three half circles by tying a string around a pencil to achieve shelf depths of 7½", 6", and 4½". Sand the cut-out pieces.

Assemble the shelf pieces and spools with epoxy by referring to the photograph for placement. Let the epoxy dry. Paint the assembled shelf with two coats of FV, letting the paint dry between coats. Apply the varnish and let dry.

—*Designed by Martha Sutyak*

SILVER "HAPPY HOLIDAYS" GARLAND

Shown on pages 94 and 102.
The garland is 78" long.

YOU WILL NEED

Walnut Hollow 2¾" wooden letters
Duncan Precious Metals acrylic paint:
    Sterling Silver AM401 (SS)
Paintbrush: #10 flat
Package of silver-leaf sheets and adhesive
Spray sealer
52—5/16" silver screw eyes
5' length of silver chain
18-gauge silver-color copper wire
13—15mm silver-washed fluted beads
Jewelry pliers

INSTRUCTIONS

Paint the wooden letters with SS; let the paint dry. Apply an even coat of the adhesive to the letters; let the adhesive dry until it is tacky. Press the silver-leaf sheets onto the adhesive. Apply a coat of aerosol sealer.

Determine the screw-eye locations on each letter, measuring 2" from the bottom edge. Insert a screw eye into each location.

Determine the amount of chain needed to go between each letter, and clip the needed length of chain. Open the end chain link, and insert the link through the screw eye on the letter. Use the pliers to close the chain link. Join the remaining letters.

To connect the words, cut two 2" lengths of chain and wire. Insert a wire through each bead, and use pliers to form loops on the ends. Join the loops to the chains.

Cut eight 2" lengths of wire and insert through the beads. Make loops at each end of the wires. Alternate beads and chains on each side of the garland until you have reached your desired length.

—*Designed by Dawn Anderson*

Presents
WITH
Presence

Show your affection with handcrafted gifts such
as our dancing angel. You won't need a lot of skill or
shopping carts full of materials to craft impressive
presents with a personal touch. Jellies and jams straight
from your kitchen are perfect for a teacher or
neighbor or as hostess gifts. Add jar toppers cross-stitched
on perforated paper for a decorative touch.
Instructions begin on page 114.

A simple wooden angel spreads her tiny wings and dances with joy.

She's bound to bring a smile—and maybe even a giggle—to everyone she greets.

Interesting (but easy) crochet stitches and fluffy chenille yarns combine in an

afghan loaded with texture and warmth. Instructions begin on page 116.

Felted wool has a heavy, old-world feel. It also doesn't ravel and fray, making appliqué quick and easy. We'll tell you how to felt the wool and then apply a design to a purchased scarf (above). Instructions begin at right.

FELTING WOOL

Felting the wool gives it a loftier look and reduces fraying. To felt the wool, launder it in the washing machine with detergent in hot water on the regular cycle, and rinse it in cold water. Dry the wool in the dryer on the hottest setting, adding a fabric-softener sheet to reduce static. The change in the temperature and the agitation of the washing machine cause the wool fibers to mat together or felt.

The wool will shrink by about one-third in the felting process (4" or more per yard), tightening the weave. Washing wool this way makes it more durable and removes fabric finishes that may have been added at the mill. It also removes dry-cleaning chemicals, oil, and perspiration from garments that have been worn.

FELTED-WOOL POINSETTIA SCARF

Shown at right.

YOU WILL NEED

Tracing paper
Purchased scarf
Felted-wool scraps: white, red, dark green, and light green (or ⅛ yard of each)
Rayon embroidery floss: white, red, green, and gold
Embroidery needle

INSTRUCTIONS

Note: *Vary the colors of wool to match the color of your purchased scarf; or, make your own scarf from felted wool, fringing the short edges.*

Trace the patterns; cut out. From the white wool, cut one poinsettia. From the red wool, cut three berries. From the green wools, cut one light leaf and two dark leaves.

Pin the wool pieces on the scarf. Embroider them with two plies of floss, using the pattern lines as a guide. Use matching floss to sew the poinsettia and leaves to the scarf with running stitches. To attach the berries, use red floss to make French knots, wrapping the floss twice around the needle. Make gold French knots at the center of the poinsettia. Stem-stitch the stems with green floss.

—*Designed by Beverly Rivers*

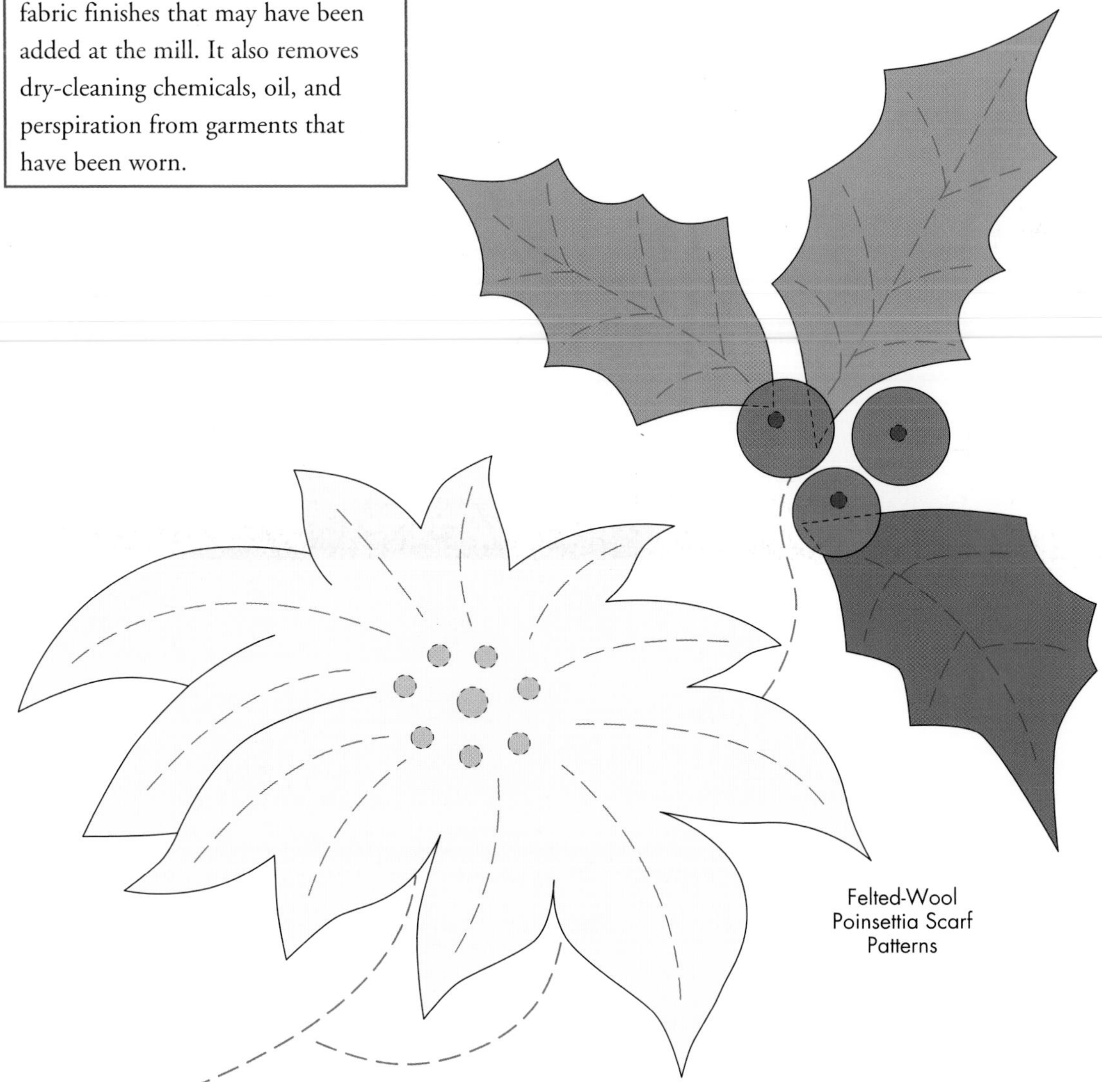

Felted-Wool
Poinsettia Scarf
Patterns

JAM JAR TAGS
Shown on page 108-109.

YOU WILL NEED

For each tag
4×4" square 14-count antique white
   perforated paper
Cotton embroidery floss
3×3" square of cream stiffened felt
3×3" square of red stiffened felt
Crafts glue
Scissors and pinking shears

INSTRUCTIONS

Center and stitch the desired design on
the perforated paper. Use three plies of
floss unless otherwise specified on the
chart. Trim the perforated paper two
squares beyond the stitching. Center
and glue the stitched square on the
cream felt square. With scissors, trim
the felt ¼" beyond the paper. Center
and glue the cream felt on the red felt
square. With pinking shears, trim the
red felt ¼" beyond the cream felt.

—*Designed by Karen Taylor*

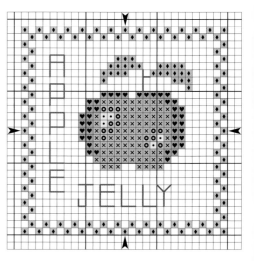

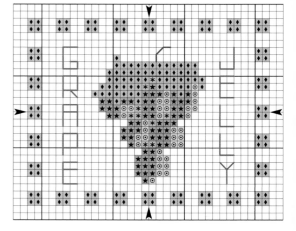

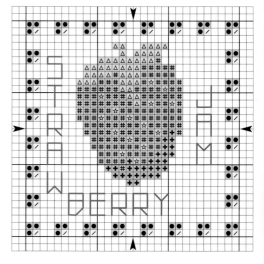

Anchor		DMC	
1006	☒	304	Christmas red
042	◉	309	Rose
100	★	327	Antique violet
1025	▦	347	Salmon
102	✳	550	Deep violet
098	◉	553	Medium violet
227	△	701	Christmas green
301	╱	744	Yellow
1005	♥	816	Garnet
047	✚	817	Deep coral
1012	•	948	Peach
246	◆	986	Forest green
923	●	3818	Emerald
306	☆	3820	Straw

BACKSTITCH (2X)

100	╱	327	Antique violet – grape lettering
371	╱	433	Chestnut – apple and grape stems
1005	╱	816	Garnet – apple lettering
923	╱	3818	Emerald – strawberry lettering

Apple stitch count: *29 high x 29 wide*
Apple finished design sizes:
14-count fabric – 2 x 2 inches
16-count fabric – 1⅞ x 1⅞ inches
18-count fabric – 1⅝ x 1⅝ inches
Grapes stitch count: *26 high x 34 wide*
Grapes finished design sizes:
14-count fabric – 1⅞ x 2⅜ inches
16-count fabric – 1⅝ x 2⅛ inches
18-count fabric – 1⅜ x 1⅞ inches
Strawberry stitch count: *30 high x 30 wide*
Strawberry finished design sizes:
14-count fabric – 2⅛ x 2⅛ inches
16-count fabric – 1⅞ x 1⅞ inches
18-count fabric – 1⅔ x 1⅔ inches

DANCING ANGEL FIGURINE

Shown on pages 108 and 110.

YOU WILL NEED

Patterns on page 116

Tracing paper

6×9" piece of 1" pine

3×6" piece of ⅛" Baltic birch plywood

4×4" piece of 2" pine

2¼"-diameter wooden wheel

½"-diameter wooden ball

15" piece of ⁵⁄₁₆"-diameter dowel (for the legs)

15" piece of ¼"-diameter dowel (for the arms and neck)

Scrollsaw and #5R blade

Table saw or radial-arm saw

Drill and ¼" and ⁵⁄₁₆" bits

100- and 150-grit sandpaper

Woodworker's glue

Wood sealer

Paintbrushes: 1" flat, #2 liner, and #4 filbert

Delta Ceramcoat Colors: Adobe 2046 (AO), Black 2506 (BK), Burnt Sienna 2030 (BS), Fleshtone 2019 (FL), Light Ivory 2401 (LI), Pine Green (PN), Red Iron Oxide 2020 (RI), and Trail Tan 2435 (TR)

Transparent tape, ¾"-wide

DecoArt Weathered Wood crackle medium

Gold-leaf sheets and adhesive size

Stiff brush (to use with the gold leaf)

Antiquing medium

7½" length of 16-gauge wire

5-minute epoxy

Needle-nose pliers

¾×12" strip of fabric

INSTRUCTIONS

Trace the angel outline onto tracing paper. Copy the outline of the angel's dress onto 1" pine (actual thickness: ¾") and the wings onto ⅛" Baltic birch plywood. Cut out the shapes with a scrollsaw, using a #5R blade. Using a tablesaw or a radial-arm saw, cut a 3×3" square from the 2" pine (actual thickness: 1½"). Cut a 1¼" length from the ¼" dowel (for the angel's neck), then cut the remaining piece and the ⁵⁄₁₆" dowel in half (arms and legs). Drill all holes where shown on the pattern.

Prepare the wood

Sand all surfaces with 100- and then 150-grit sandpaper. Remove the sanding dust with a tack cloth. Attach the wheel to the top of the base with woodworker's glue; let the glue dry. Apply wood sealer to all surfaces, and let the sealer dry. Sand again with 150-grit sandpaper, and wipe clean with a tack cloth.

Base-coat the angel

Using a 1" flat brush and RI, base-coat the dress, the base, the wings, and the arms (leave ¾" at one end of each arm for hands). Let the paint dry.

Measure and mark a line ¾" from the bottom edge of the dress, and place the bottom edge of a piece of tape along this line. Extend the tape around the sides of the dress, and press firmly along the edges so paint does not seep underneath. Leave the tape on until the crackling process is completed.

Crackle the paint

Using a 1" flat brush, apply a thin coat of crackle medium to the dress. Let the medium dry according to the manufacturer's directions. Brush TR over the dress, and while the paint is still wet, stroke LI here and there. To further create an aged look, rub your finger randomly over the wet crackled paint, removing it to show the base-coat color. Remove the tape, and allow the paint to dry. Dry-brush TR and then LI over the arms.

Apply gold leaf

To apply the gold leaf, brush the adhesive size over the wings, the wheel on the base, and the red band on the dress. Let the size dry until it's tacky. Handle the sheets of gold leaf with tissue paper, and press them onto the size. Tap them in place with a stiff brush. Let the leaf dry.

Paint the details

Using a 1" flat brush, base-coat the face, the hands, and the legs FL. Dilute AO with water 1:1, and paint the cheeks with a #4 filbert brush. Mix FL and BS 1:1, and dilute the mixture with water to ink consistency. Use a #2 liner brush to paint the nose with the diluted BS. Dot the eyes BK.

Dilute PN with water to ink consistency and, using a #2 liner brush, paint the long stem lines on the dress. Paint the leaves PN with a #4 filbert brush. Dot the flowers AO using the handle end of a brush. Let the dots dry, and then apply smaller RI dots where shown on the pattern.

Finish the angel

Apply antiquing medium to all surfaces except the face; remove the excess medium, and let it dry thoroughly. Sand spots of paint from the fronts of the wings and the back of the dress. (Glue and epoxy won't bond permanently to painted or varnished surfaces.) Epoxy the wings to the dress, the neck into the head and the dress, and the arms and the legs into the dress. Cut five 1½" lengths of 16-gauge wire, and use needle-nose pliers to bend one end of each piece as shown. Epoxy the wires into the head. Let the epoxy set. Tie the strip of fabric around the neck.

—*Designed by Shara Reiner*

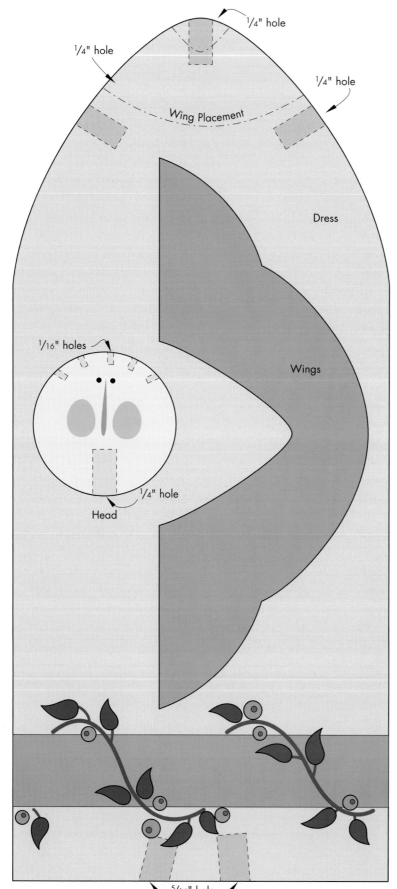

¼" hole

¼" hole

¼" hole

Wing Placement

Dress

Wings

¹⁄₁₆" holes

¼" hole

Head

⁵⁄₁₆" hole

Dancing Angel Figurine Patterns

GREENS IN THE SNOW CHENILLE AFGHAN

Shown on page 111.
The finished afghan measures
approximately 42×49".

YOU WILL NEED

Lion Brand Yarn Chenille Sensations: 12 skeins
   of antique white (#098), and 10 skeins
   of forest green (#131)
Size 6/G aluminum crochet hook or size
   to obtain gauge
9 yarn bobbins

CHOCHETABBREVIATIONS

beg—beginning
bpdc—back post double crochet
ch—chain
cont—continue
dc—double crochet
foll—follow(s)(ing)
fpdc—front post double crochet
inc—increase
pat—pattern
rep—repeat
rem—remain(ing)
rnd—round
rs—right side
sc—single crochet
sk—skip; skipping
sl st—slip stitch
sp—space
st(s)—stitch(es)
yo—yarn over

Gauge: In dc and color pat, 13 sts=4";
9 rows=5". In body pat, 15 sts and
9 rows=4".

INSTRUCTIONS

Note: *Refer to Crochet Basics beginning*
on page 156 for instructions on the chain
stitch, single crochet, and double crochet.

Stitches

Front post double crochet: Yarn over, insert the hook around the post of the next stitch from the front to the back and to the front again, draw up a loop (yarn over, draw through 2 loops on hook) twice.

Back post double crochet: Yarn over, insert the hook around the post of the next stitch from the back to the front and to the back again, draw up a loop (yarn over, draw through 2 loops on hook) twice.

Note: To change color while working in double crochet, in last st before new color, dc with present color until 2 lps rem on hook; with new color, yo and complete the dc. When working Chart 1, carry the color not in use loosely along the top of the last row of sts, working over them as you go. For Chart 2, separate bobbins are recommended for each snowflake.

Foundation

Begin the afghan with the lower edge using green, ch 156.

Foundation (RS): Sc in second ch from hook and in each ch across—155 sts. Fasten off green.

Row 2: With the RS facing, join white with sl st in first sc at right edge; ch 3 (counts as dc); dc in each sc across; turn.

Row 3: Ch 3 (counts as dc), bpdc in each of next 4 sts; * fpdc in each of next 5 sts **, bpdc in each of next 5 sts; rep from * across,

ending last rep at **, bpdc in each of next 4 sts, dc in turning ch; turn.

Row 4: Ch 3 (counts as dc), fpdc in each of next 4 sts; * bpdc in each of next 5 sts **, fpdc in each of next 5 sts; rep from * across, ending last rep at **, fpdc in each of next 4 sts, dc in turning ch; turn. Fasten off.

Body Pattern

Row 1: With the RS facing, join green with sl st in top of turning ch at the right edge. Ch 1, sc in same sp as join and in next st (keeping last lp of each st on hook, work 3 dc in next st, yo and draw through all 4 lps on hook—bobble made); * sc in each of next 4 sts, bobble in next st; rep from * across, ending sc in last 2 sts. Next, fasten off.

Row 2: With the RS facing, join white with sl st in first sc at right edge. Ch 3 (counts as dc); dc in each sc and bobble across; turn.

Rows 3–7: Rep Foundation Rows 3–4.

Row 8: Rep Foundation Row 3. Fasten off.

Rep Rows 1–7 of body pat for 4 times more; rep rows 1–4 again. Fasten off.

With the RS facing, join green with sl st in top of turning ch at right edge. Ch 1, sc in same sp as join; sc in each st across. Fasten off.

For side edging (work along each side edge): With the RS facing, join green with sl st at right edge. Ch 1, work 65 sc evenly spaced along edge;

turn. Ch 1, sc in each sc across. Fasten off.

Border

Border (work along each side edge): With the RS facing, join green with sl st in side edging. Ch 3 (counts as dc); work 158 dc evenly spaced along edge=159 sts; turn.

Rows 1–3: Follow Chart 1, below.

Row 4: With green ch 3 to begin, dc in each dc across; turn.

Rows 5–9: Ch 3 (counts as dc); follow Chart 2 below, beginning at A and working to C; then rep B–C.

Row 10: Rep Row 4.

Rows 11–13: Follow Chart 1, below.

Row 14: Rep Row 4, dec 2 sts—157 sts.

Row 15: Ch 1, sc in each of first 5 sts; * ch 2, sk 1 st, in next st (2 dc, ch 2, 2 dc=shell made), ch 2, sk 1 st, sc in each of next 5 sts; rep from * across; turn.

Row 16: Ch 1, sc in each of first 4 sc; * ch 3, sk ch-2 sp (shell in ch-2 sp of next shell=shell in shell made), ch 3, sk 1 sc, sc in each of next 3 sc; rep from * across, ending sc in last sc; turn.

Row 17: Ch 1, sc in each of first 3 sc; * ch 4, sk ch-3 sp, shell in shell, ch 4, sk 1 sc, sc in next sc; rep from * across, ending sc in last 2 sc. Fasten off. Rep Border for opposite edge.

—*Designed by Ann E. Smith*

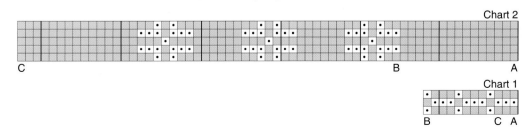

Memories
OF CHRISTMAS
Past

Relive yesteryear's holidays with trims that evoke

Victorian days. Garden bell cloches (opposite) come indoors

for the winter as covers for nostalgic winter scenes. Place them

on platters or cake plates for a stunning display. Bottle-brush

trees, old-fashioned figurines, and vintage Christmas

tree decorations also recall the charm of simpler, more

romantic times. Instructions begin on page 126.

Tell your family's story on a tree draped with photos and quaint Christmas images (opposite). Frame photocopies of prints between acetate, bind them with copper-foil tape, and top them with beaded hangers. A button-haired angel with primitive charm stays earthbound with wings of wood. Give the shapely architectural trim a wash of white paint to complement the antique look of this folk-art sculpture. Instructions begin on page 126.

Two Victorian favorites—decoupage and crazy quilts—come together

on a memory book made from sentimental cards and papers (above).

Painted dots and dashes simulate the stitching between the patterns.

Old cards get a new lease on life as dainty shoe ornaments (opposite). Lace them

together moccasin-style with shimmery ribbon, and tie them to a

garland or tree. Instructions begin on page 127.

Mold curly-haired lambs (above) from pliable modeling clay,
and complete them with wavy wool coats and cinnamon-stick legs.
The season's favorite words hide in the alphabet of a cross-stitch stocking inspired
by traditional sampler motifs (opposite). Instructions begin on page 130.

SNOW-SCENE DOME
Shown on page 118-119.

YOU WILL NEED

Antique and new Santas, angels, tree
 ornaments, or other holiday collectibles
Miniature trees (available at miniatures shops)
Purchased glass dome (available at crafts,
 hobby, and garden-decor stores)
Cake plate, serving platter, or other round base
 that will fit beneath your dome
Tacky wax (available at miniatures shops)
Polyester quilt batting
Clear crystal glitter

INSTRUCTIONS

Choose favorite items from your
collections that will fit under the
dome. Arrange them on the base with
two or three miniature trees. When
you're pleased with the arrangement,
use tacky wax to hold each item in
place on the base.

Tuck small tufts of quilt batting
around the items, and sprinkle the
batting with glitter to suggest frost on
the snow. Put the dome cover in place.

—Designed by Beverly Rivers

FAMILY-TREE ORNAMENTS
Shown on page 120.

YOU WILL NEED

Family photographs
Old greeting cards, die cuts, and
 decorative papers
¼"-wide copper-foil tape
Clear acetate or Mylar film
Fine-point awl or a small nail and a hammer
Needle-nose pliers
Beads
Medium-weight copper wire

INSTRUCTIONS

Copy your family photos on a color
copier (even if you want black-and-
white photos). The color copier will
produce a sharper image with better
gradations of black, white, and gray.
If you'd like a sepia tone, set the color
copier on "one color" and choose tan
as the color.

Cut the photocopy to the desired
size or use a greeting-card image or a
die cut with a backing of heavy paper
or card stock. If you use die cuts, place
them on decorative paper for the
background; cut the decorative paper
and backing to the desired size.
Next, cut two clear acetate shapes the
same size to cover the front and back
of the photocopy. Sandwich them
together, and cover the edges with
copper foil tape.

For the hanger, us an awl or a nail
and a hammer to punch a hole in each
upper corner about ¼" in from each
edge. Cut an 8" length of copper wire;
push one end of the wire through one
of the holes and, with needle-nose
pliers, twist it to secure. (If desired,
leave enough wire at the end to thread
on a decorative bead before twisting.)
Add beads to the hanger, and push the
other end through the opposite hole;
secure the wire with a twist, adding a
bead if desired.

—Designed by Beverly Rivers

CHRISTMAS-CARD SHOES

Shown on page 123.

YOU WILL NEED

Tracing paper
Christmas cards
Spray adhesive
Clear acetate
Hole punch
Cord or ribbon

INSTRUCTIONS

Trace the patterns onto tracing paper. Cut out the pattern pieces.

For the shoe soles, use spray adhesive to glue two pieces of card material together with the wrong sides facing. Cut out one sole for each shoe. If the card material is heavy, a single layer may be sufficient. Cut a shoe top from one layer of card material. To reverse the direction of the shoe, flip the pattern pieces over before tracing. From clear acetate, cut one shoe sole and one shoe top.

Work with the corresponding card and acetate pieces as one; do not glue them together. Position the shoe tops over the shoe soles, matching the marks on the patterns; punch one hole at each mark. Continue punching equally spaced holes around both shoes. Use cord or ribbon to lace the shoe tops to the bottoms, beginning and ending at the back of the sole and leaving 10" tails for tying.

—*Designed by Beverly Rivers*

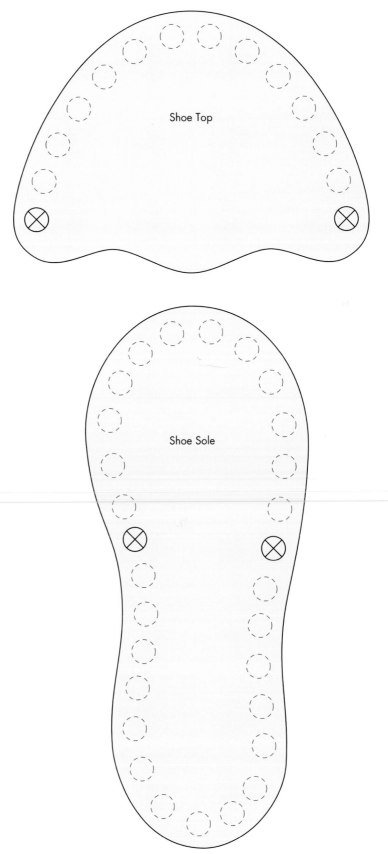

Shoe Top

Shoe Sole

Christmas-Card Shoes Patterns

VINTAGE ANGEL

Shown on page 121.
The doll is 31" tall and has
31"-wide wings.

YOU WILL NEED

½ yard of tan muslin (for the body)
½ yard of ivory muslin (for the dress lining)
⅔ yard of lace (for the dress)
Paper
Sewing needle and matching thread
Polyester fiberfill
⅜"-wide craft stick
½ yard of 1/16"-wide ivory satin ribbon
1 yard of ¼"-wide ivory cotton ribbon or
    seam tape
Cotton embroidery floss: ivory and tan
25-30 assorted buttons
1×4×30" pine
Scrollsaw
100- and 150-grit sandpaper
Tack cloth
Ivory acrylic paint
1" sponge brush
Matte-finish varnish
Sawtooth hanger

INSTRUCTIONS

Enlarge the patterns onto paper; cut them out. The outlines are the sewing lines. The measurements for other pieces include ¼" seam allowances. Sew them with right sides together, using ¼" seams.

Sew the body

Trace the body and arm patterns onto doubled tan muslin. Sew on the traced lines, leaving an opening at the bottom of the body and the top of each arm. Cut out the body and arms ¼" beyond the sewn lines, and clip the curves.

Turn the body and the arms right side out. Use a pencil to lightly transfer the facial details onto one side of the head. Stuff the head firmly with polyester fiberfill. Insert the craft stick into the neck and about half way up the back side of the head. Finish stuffing the body and the arms with polyester fiberfill. Hand-sew the bottom opening on the body closed. Turn over the raw edges on the arms, and hand-sew the arms to the body. Use three plies of tan floss to stitch the mouth and the nose. Use ivory floss to sew on the button eyes and hair.

Assemble the dress

From the ivory muslin, cut two 8×24" rectangles for the dress lining. Sew the rectangles together at the long edges, leaving a 2" opening on each side for the arm holes. Sew the 8" edges together on the armhole end, leaving a 2" opening at the center for the neck. Turn the lining right side out. With scissors, cut a 2"-deep V-shape into the 2" front neck opening. Turn under the raw edges and finger-press. Slip the lining on the angel.

From the lace fabric, cut two 8×24" rectangles for the dress and two 10×6" rectangles for the sleeves. Sew the 8" edges of the dress rectangles together at one end, leaving an 2" opening in the center for the neck (shoulder seams). Center and sew the 6" edge of one sleeve rectangle to a shoulder seam. Sew the other sleeve to the other shoulder in the same manner. Sew the long edges of one sleeve rectangle together; continue sewing down the long edge of the dress rectangle (underarm seam). Repeat with the other sleeve and dress rectangles.

Dress the doll

Weave the 1/16" ribbon through the edges of the neck opening of the dress lace. Slip the dress on, and pull the ribbon tightly to gather the dress around the angel's neck and tie the ribbon in a bow. Tie a 24" length of ¼" ribbon around the angel under her arms to form a dress bodice, and tie in a bow. Wrap the remaining ¼" ribbon around the neck and tie in a bow.

Paint the wings

Use a scrollsaw to cut the wings from the 1" pine. Sand the cutout with 100- and then 150-grit sandpaper. Remove the sanding dust with a tack cloth. Prepare a 1:1 mixture of ivory paint and water. With the sponge brush, apply the mixture on the front and back surfaces, leaving the cut edges bare. Brush on varnish and let the varnish dry. Using six plies of embroidery floss, hand-sew the wings to the angel by sewing into the angel body and wrapping the floss over the wings. Attach a sawtooth hanger in the center of the back of the wings.

—Designed by Ruth Cox

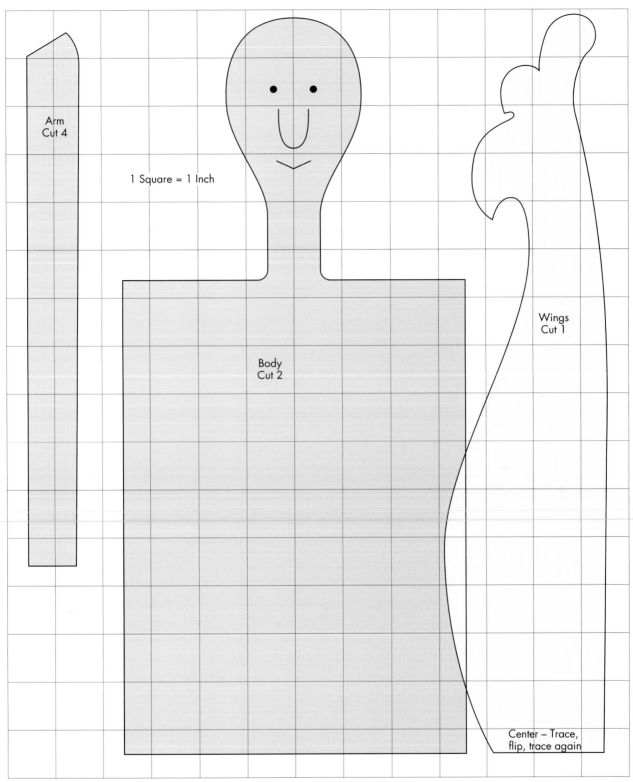

Arm
Cut 4

1 Square = 1 Inch

Body
Cut 2

Wings
Cut 1

Center – Trace,
flip, trace again

Vintage Angel Patterns

CHRISTMAS SAMPLER STOCKING

Shown on page 124.

YOU WILL NEED

21×14" piece of 14-count natural/rustico
   Aida cloth
Cotton embroidery floss
Erasable fabric marking pen
19×12" piece of fusible fleece
1 yard of 45"-wide Christmas print fabric
1¼ yard of ⅛"-diameter cording

INSTRUCTIONS

Center and stitch the design from the chart onto the fabric. Use three plies of floss to work the stitches unless otherwise specified. Press the stitchery from the back.

Center and fuse the fleece to the back of the stitched piece following the manufacturer's instructions. Use the erasable marker to draw the stocking outline as indicated by the dashed line on the chart. Cut out the stocking ½" beyond the marked line.

Use the stocking as a pattern to cut a matching back and two lining pieces. Cut a 1⅝×5" hanging strip from the Christmas fabric. Also cut and piece strips to make a 1⅝×45" piping strip from the Christmas fabric.

Center the cording lengthwise on the wrong side of the piping strip. Fold the fabric around the cording with the raw edges together. Use a zipper foot to sew through both layers close to the cording. Baste the piping around the sides and foot of the stocking front with the raw edges even.

Press the long edges of the hanging strip under ½", fold in half lengthwise, and topstitch. Fold the strip in half to form a loop. Tack the ends inside the top right side of the stocking.

With right sides together, using the zipper foot, sew the stocking front to the back with a ½" seam allowance,

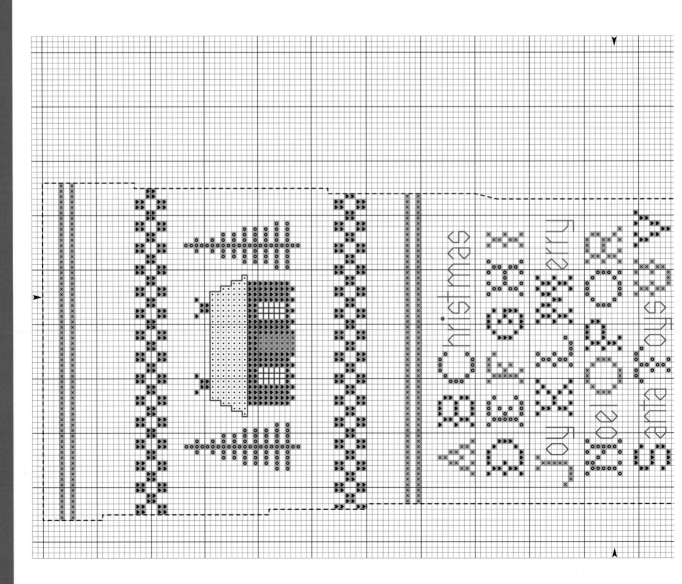

leaving the top edge open. Trim the seam allowance to ¼". For curves, clip the piping seam allowance frequently until the piping lies flat. Turn right side out and press. With right sides together, sew the stocking lining together, leaving the top edge open and an opening in the foot; do not turn. Slip the stocking inside the lining. Stitch the stocking to the lining at the top edges with right sides together; turn. Slip-stitch the opening closed. Tuck the lining into the stocking and press carefully.

—*Designed by Jim Williams*

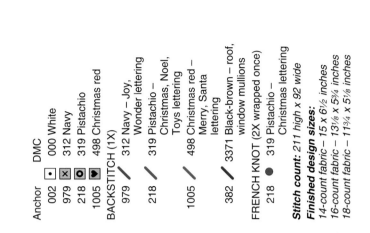

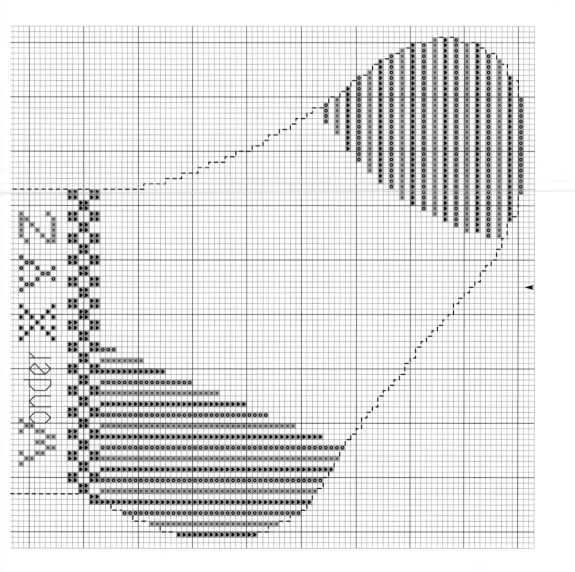

CRAZY-QUILT ALBUM

Shown on page 122.
The album is 10×12".

YOU WILL NEED

Walnut Hollow Wooden Album #3700
100- and 150-grit sandpaper
Tack cloth
Aleene's Enhancers: All-Purpose Primer EN104
    and Satin Varnish EN102
Aleene's Premium-Coat Acrylic Paints:
    Buttercream OC216 (BC), Deep Green
    OC140 (DG), Dusty Green OC141 (GN),
    Gold OC301 (GD), True Red OC103 (TR),
    and White OC173 (WH)
Paintbrushes: 1" sponge, #8 flat brush, #2
    liner, and spatter brush or old toothbrush
Christmas cards or wrapping paper
Aleene's Instant Decoupage Glue Sealer
Aleene's Matte-Finish Varnish
Tracing and transfer paper
Cotton swabs
Tulip Pearl Fabric Paint: Snow White
    65043 (SW)

INSTRUCTIONS

Disassemble the album. Sand all surfaces of the album components with 100- and then 150-grit sandpaper. Remove the sanding dust with a tack cloth. Apply All-Purpose Primer to all surfaces, following the manufacturer's instructions; let the primer dry.

Use the sponge brush to base-coat all surfaces of the pieces with two coats of BC; let paint dry.

Cut the Christmas cards or paper into irregular shapes; cut more shapes than you'll need to cover the right front album piece. Lay out the shapes on a flat work surface in a color arrangement that pleases you.

Select a place to begin on the right front album piece. Apply decoupage medium to the wood where the shape will be placed and onto the back of the shape. Place the shape on the album. Brush the decoupage medium on the top of the shape, smoothing out any air bubbles with moist fingertips. Work away from the first shape, cutting the second card to fit beside the first shape with a slight overlap. Repeat the decoupaging steps with each shape until the right front album piece is completely covered. Brush on two or three more coats of the decoupage medium for even coverage. Let medium dry.

Trace the pattern onto tracing paper. Position the pattern on the left front album piece, and transfer it with transfer paper. To create holly, use the #8 flat brush to float GN on inside

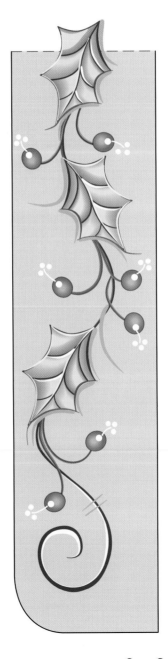

Crazy-Quilt Album

edges of the leaves and to float in vein lines. When the paint is dry, repeat the steps with a float of DG. Use the #2 liner brush to outline the holly leaves with DG and then with WH. Paint the stems DG, and highlight with WH. Using GD, highlight around one edge of each leaf and here and there on the stems.

For the large center berries, float TR. Keeping the color along the inside edge, float WH on one side of each berry. Add a TR dot on the light side. Paint a WH stamen with three small dots on the end.

Use a cotton swab to paint the small berries TR. While the paint is still wet, use a damp cotton swab to lift off some of the paint from the center of the small berries. Finish as for the large center berries.

On the front of the album, paint SW lines that resemble embroidery stitches between the decoupage shapes; let the paint dry.

Float GD around all edges of each album piece, including the decoupaged front. Use a cotton swab to rub GD around the sides of the album pieces. Thin GD with water to ink consistency; using a spatter brush, lightly spatter (flyspeck) all surfaces of the album pieces.

When the paint is completely dry, apply one or two coats of satin varnish; let the varnish dry.

—*Designed by Inga Johns*

WOOLLY SHEEP
Shown on pages 125.

YOU WILL NEED
Sculpey Polymer Clay
Cinnamon Sticks
Glue gun and hotmelt adhesive
Wavy or curly wool
Black acrylic paint for face
Artist's fine liner brush
¼"-wide ribbon (optional)

INSTRUCTIONS
You can make the sheep any size that works for your display. The instructions here are for finished sheep that are 4" tall and 4½" from nose to tail.

For the head, pinch off enough clay to make a 1½"-diameter ball. Roll it into a cone-shaped egg. At the wide end of the egg shape, use your thumbs to make triangular ears. Smooth all surfaces of the clay.

For the body, pinch off a 2½- to 3"-diameter ball, and shape it into a tube with rounded ends. At one end pull up a ½"-tall neck.

Press the head onto the neck, and smooth the seam. Insert the cinnamon-stick legs into the body. Stand the body on a baking sheet, and smooth all edges of the clay. Bake in a 275-degree oven for 15 minutes per ¼" of body thickness or according to the manufacturer's instructions. (If you use another clay, follow the manufacturer's directions for baking.) Turn off the oven, and let it cool completely before removing the sheep from the oven.

Using hotmelt adhesive, cover the body with small pieces of the wavy or curly wool. Paint the face details with black acrylic paint, using a very fine artist's liner brush to make thin lines for the features.

If desired, tie a ribbon bow around the neck.

—*Designed by Beverly Rivers*

Make the head and the body, then join the two. Pinch the clay to form the ears. Insert the cinnamon sticks, and bake to a hard finish in your oven.

THROUGH THE EYES
OF A *Child*

Giggles will ring through the house when the kids gather
for holiday crafting. Whether they're making ornaments
for their very own tree (right) or silly pencil toppers
(below) to give as gifts, there will never be a shortage of
imagination and energy. Instructions begin on page 141.

Half-pint milk cartons, graham crackers, and canned frosting

make constructing a sweet village (above) a snap.

Cookie cutters, air-dry foam, and glue-on trims turn out ornaments

that look bakery-fresh (opposite). Use the same materials to shape the

"buggy" critters. String candy and cereal on gold cord to form icicles that

look good enough to eat. Instructions begin on page 141.

Pair up prestretched artist's canvas and gilded frames, then let the kids go to town with acrylic paints, creating a gallery of charmingly naive artwork (above). Check out these insects (opposite)—they're fun, friendly, and furry. Give them a shake, and they'll jingle as they move. Instructions begin on page 144.

Make Christmas wishes known to everyone. Transfer kids' letters to Santa and their Christmas artwork onto holiday shirts (above) using special photo-transfer paper, then embellish the shirts with buttons and washable trims. Instructions begin opposite.

specialize in custom T-shirts to see if they offer a transfer service. Sew bows, bells, buttons, and other trims to the T-shirt as desired.

COOKIES THAT LAST
Shown on page 135 and 136.

YOU WILL NEED
Rolling pin and cutting board
Assorted colors of Crayola Model Magic
   modeling compound
Simple cookie-cutter shapes
Plastic straw
Beads, glue-on gemstones, chenille stems,
   glitter, and scraps of rickrack, lace,
   cocktail straws, and colored paper
Permanent marking pens (optional)
Thick white crafts glue
15" lengths of ¼"-wide grosgrain ribbon
   for hanging loops

INSTRUCTIONS
Roll out the modeling compound on the cutting board. Carefully cut out shapes with the cookie cutters. Use the plastic straw to make a hole at the top of each shape for a hanging loop. To make tiny candles for tree boughs, cut ⅜" lengths of cocktail straws; use yellow modeling compound to form a flame on one end of each straw. Press the straws into the tree.

Decorate the ornaments as desired by pressing beads, gemstones, chenille stems, glitter, rickrack, and/or lace into the modeling compound. Cut simple clothing shapes from colored paper for bears. Let the ornaments dry completely. Use glue to reattach the decorations if they become loose during the drying process. If desired, use permanent marking pens to add details such as the small dots on the trees. Thread grosgrain ribbon through the hole at the top of each ornament; tie the ends into a bow for hanging.

SANTA WISH-LIST SHIRTS
Shown opposite.

YOU WILL NEED
8½×11" sheet of white paper
Colored marking pens
White T-shirt
Assorted bows, bells, buttons, and other
   washable trims (optional)

INSTRUCTIONS
Ask your child to draw a picture and write a Christmas wish list on a sheet of white paper. *Note: We used marking pens, but colored pencils and crayons also work. The brighter and stronger the colors, the better.*

To make a fabric transfer, take the finished artwork to a photocopy shop, and have it prepared for use as a T-shirt transfer. The resulting transfer should be a mirror image of the original artwork to ensure the handwriting transfers properly.

Next, have the transfer heat-set onto a white T-shirt, following the manufacturer's directions. You may also wish to check with shops that

HOLIDAY PENCIL TOPPERS
Shown on page 134 and below.

YOU WILL NEED

Tracing paper
Pencils
Crafts glue
Hole punch

For the Angel:
1—1"-diameter plastic foam ball
3—4"-diameter circles of blue tulle
Metallic paper
Hole punch
Pink chenille stem
Halloween spiderweb material
Silver-glitter chenille stem
2 whole cloves
1 pink seed bead

For the Santa:
1—1"-diameter plastic foam ball
Scrap of red wrapping paper
2 tiny jingle bells
White thick-and-thin chenille stem
2 whole cloves
¼"-diameter red pom-pom
Black chenille stem

For the Snowman:
2—1"-diameter plastic foam balls
2 whole cloves
Toothpick
Orange marker
Bright shoelace for the scarf
Thin twigs for the arms and mouth
White chenille stem
Fresh, silk, or plastic evergreen branch
    and red beads
Glove for the hat and a ¼" white
    pom-pom

INSTRUCTIONS

Trace the Santa hat and angel wing patterns onto tracing paper and cut out the patterns.

Angel Pencil Topper
Push the lead end of the pencil about one-third of the way into the plastic-foam ball. Center the three layers of tulle over the eraser. Hold the tulle tightly gathered around the eraser. Glue the ball to the eraser end of the pencil over the tulle.

Trace the wing pattern onto metallic paper; cut it out. Use a hole punch to make two holes in the wings, referring to the pattern for placement. Fold the pink chenille stem into a U shape; thread the ends through the holes in the wings with the ends at the front. Place the wings on the angel's back and twist the pink stem around the pencil slightly below the head. Bend the stem to form elbows and hands.

Use a 1×6" piece of Halloween spiderweb material for the hair. Pinch the web together for the center part and glue to top of head. Pull the web to the back of the head and trim the ends evenly.

Form a halo at one end of the glitter chenille stem to fit on the angel's head. Bend the straight portion of the stem at a right angle from the halo. Trim the stem 1" from the halo. Push the halo stem into the head.

Push cloves into the head for eyes. For the mouth, push the pink seed bead into the face; glue it in place if necessary.

Santa Pencil Topper
Push the lead end of the pencil about one-third of the way into the plastic-foam ball. Glue the ball to the eraser end of the pencil.

Trace the hat pattern onto red paper; cut it out. Form the paper into a cone shape, and tape it together. Glue the hat to Santa's head. Glue a bell to the hat tip.

Cut one thin and two thick portions from the white chenille stem. For the beard, slightly bend one thick portion to curve around the bottom of the face and push the ends into the head. Bend the second thick portion, and push the ends into the head for the hatband. Bend the thin portion in half and push the fold into the center of the face. Curl the ends to form the mustache. Glue if necessary. Push cloves into the head for eyes. Glue a red pom-pom on the face for the nose. Thread the remaining bell onto the black chenille stem for the belt. Wrap and twist the belt around the pencil. Trim off the excess stem, and glue the belt in place.

Snowman Pencil Topper
Carefully push the lead end of the pencil all the way through the center of one plastic-foam ball for the body. Then push the lead end about one-third of the way into the second ball for the head. Glue the balls in position at the eraser end of the pencil, leaving ⅛" between the balls for the scarf.

Push cloves into the head for eyes. For the nose, use orange marker to color the end of the toothpick. Cut off the tip, and push it into the head. For the mouth, cut five tiny tips from the ends of the thin twigs. Push the tips into the head, forming a smile.

Cut a 6" length of shoelace. Tie the lace around the snowman's neck, and glue it in place. For the hat, cut a 2"-long section from one finger of the glove. Place the hat on the snowman's head, folding the raw edge over for the brim. Glue the pom-pom to the tip of the hat.

For the arms, push the twigs into the sides of the body. Or, cut two 1½" lengths of white chenille stem. Fold the stem lengths in half, and push the cut ends into the body. Place red beads on the pine branch, and fold an arm to hold the branch.

SNACK TIME ICICLES
Shown on page 136 and right.

YOU WILL NEED
Large-eye, blunt needle
Gold metallic thread
Fruit-flavored candy rings
Colored miniature marshmallows, dried
Fruit-flavored cereal rings
Fruit-shaped gumdrop slices and wedges

For each ornament:
Jumbo gold jingle bell
15" length of 1"-wide grosgrain ribbon

INSTRUCTIONS
Thread the needle with gold metallic thread. Leaving an 8" tail of thread, run the needle through the centers of the candy, marshmallows, and cereal pieces until the icicle is the desired length. Add the bell, and then bring the needle back through the candy and cereal pieces. Trim the thread tails to 6"; remove the needle. Center the ribbon between the thread tails, and tie the tails in a knot around the ribbon. Tie the ribbon into a bow. For a hanging loop, knot together the ends of the tails.

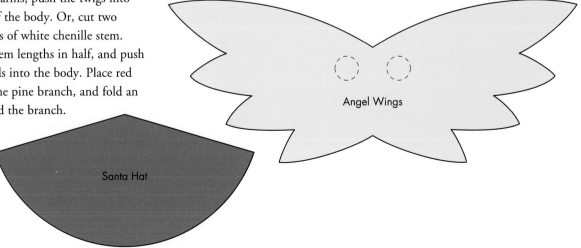

Angel Wings

Santa Hat

Holiday Pencil Toppers Patterns

GRAHAM-CRACKER VILLAGE
Shown on page 137 and below.

YOU WILL NEED

Graham crackers
Canned frosting
Half-pint milk or juice boxes, empty and clean
Assorted candies, including candy sticks,
    miniature candy canes, thin candy wafers,
    and miniature chocolate candy bars
Cake sprinkles
Cookie wafers
Fruit-flavored cereal rings

INSTRUCTIONS

For each house, you'll need seven graham cracker squares; four for the sides, two for the roof, and one for the front and back roof triangles. For the roof triangles, diagonally score a graham cracker square, and snap it along the score.

Frost one side of each roof triangle, and press it in place on the box for the house front and back, aligning the corner with the top of the box. Generously frost the sides of the box and press a graham cracker square onto each side. Frost one side of each roof piece, and press it onto the slanted box top.

Trim four candy sticks or canes to the length needed for the house corners. Press the candy sticks into the icing at the corners of the box. Frost the top of the roof and decorate it with thin candy wafers, cake sprinkles, or cookie wafers. Referring to the photo, decorate the house, using candy, cookies, and cereal loops to create windows, doors, chimneys, and flowers.

Repeat to make as many houses as desired.

EARLY IMPRESSIONS ARTWORK
Shown on pages 138.

YOU WILL NEED

Purchased artist's canvas
Paints
Paintbrushes
Ready-made frame to fit canvas

INSTRUCTIONS

Ask your child to paint a holiday picture on the prestretched artist's canvas. When the painting is dry, insert it in the readymade frame.

JINGLE BUGS ORNAMENTS
Shown on page 135 and 139.

YOU WILL NEED

Assorted colors of Crayola Model Magic
    modeling compound
Chenille stems: regular, glitter, and
    thick-and-thin
Assorted ⅜"- to 1¼"-diameter jingle bells
Small pom-poms
Paper doilies for the wings
Crafts glue

INSTRUCTIONS

Form bug shapes from modeling compound, mixing two or three colors together, if desired. Refer to the photograph on *page 139* for ideas.

For a caterpillar

Attach one end of a full-length glitter chenille stem to a 1¼"-diameter jingle bell. Thread four 1" balls of modeling compound onto the stem. Wrap the end of a stem around a pencil to curl it, and attach a ½"-diameter jingle bell to the tip. Wrap the center of a second full-length glitter chenille stem around the first one at the connection of two balls, shape into legs, and attach a ⅜"-diameter jingle bell to each end. Repeat to make two more pairs of legs. Let the modeling clay dry. Add pom-pom eyes and nose.

For a scorpion

Form modeling compound into a 1"-diameter tube, about 4½" long. Flatten one end and taper the other to a point, curving the tube slightly. Thread a 1"-diameter jingle bell onto a regular chenille stem; fold the stem in half and press both ends into the flattened end of the tube. Thread three assorted small sizes of jingle bells onto a 4" piece of glitter chenille stem; insert one end of the stem into the tapered end of the tube. Attach a ⅜"-diameter jingle bell to the other end. Curve the stem to resemble a

scorpion's tail. Shape legs and antennae from thick-and-thin chenille stems. Insert the ends into the modeling compound. Let the modeling compound dry. Add small pom-poms for eyes and nose.

For a ladybug

Form a 1"- and a 2"-diameter ball of modeling compound. Flatten each ball and press them together. Cut six 1½" lengths of glitter chenille stem, and attach a ½"-diameter jingle bell to one end of each. Insert the other ends into the large ball for legs. Cut two 3" lengths of glitter stem and attach a ⅜"-diameter jingle bell to one end of each. Press the other ends into the small ball for antennae. Cut a 2½"-diameter round doily in half and press into the top of the large ball for wings. Add ⅜"-diameter jingle bells for eyes and a ¾"-length of glitter chenille stem for the mouth. Let the modeling compound dry.

For a spider

Use a regular chenille stem to attach a 1"- and a 1¼"-diameter jingle bell. Use full-length glitter chenille stems for legs, attaching one end to the connection of the head and body. Curl the opposite ends for feet. Let the modeling compound dry. Add small pom-poms for eyes.

For a dragonfly

Form a 4½"-long tube that tapers from about ¾"-diameter at the front end to ½"-diameter at the back. Cut four 2½" lengths of thick-and-thin chenille stems and insert into the sides of the tube for wings. Cut six 1½" lengths of regular chenille stem and attach a ⅜"-diameter jingle bell to one end of each. Press the other ends into the sides of the tube for legs. Curl the end of a glitter chenille stem and insert it into the wide end of the tube for a tongue. Press jingle bells into the dragonfly's back. Let the compound dry. Add pom-poms for eyes.

—All projects designed by
Laura Holtorf Collins

TRADITIONAL
Treats

Gaily decorated cookies, hot mugs of wassail,

bright wavy ribbon candy, and ethnic favorites like molded

Scandinavian cookies and frosted rum cakes—these are

the treats that fill our minds when the holidays approach.

We've taken some of the season's favorite recipes and added

a few new twists. In our English Country Wassail (left),

baked apples bob alongside clove-studded orange slices.

Make the steamy concoction of cider and cranberry

juice with or without a bit of rum and brandy.

The recipe is on page 152.

Elaborate designs pressed into cookie dough (above) make Springerle as pretty and delicate as vintage Christmas ornaments. Add a touch of spice or chocolate to familiar cutout cookies (opposite). Bake hearty Spiced Whole Wheat Sugar Cookies for Santa and all his elves. Add dips of chocolate to dress Ginger Kids. Pipe frosting trims onto the baked cookies with a pastry bag. Recipes are on page 152.

Making ribbon candy (opposite) is an old-fashioned family affair.

It takes two people to pull and shape the candy into the serpentine bands.

Tiny eggnog- and rum-flavored cakes are packed with candied

fruits, raisins, and pecans. After baking, they're soaked in orange juice or rum

for a day or two to mellow the flavors. The recipes for Ribbon Candy,

Crystal Candy, and Rum and Eggnog Cake begin on page 154.

ENGLISH COUNTRY WASSAIL

Shown on pages 146–147.

YOU WILL NEED

Baked Apples in Brandy Sauce
3 medium oranges
2 tablespoons whole cloves (optional)
1 gallon (16 cups) apple cider or apple juice
1 quart (4 cups) cranberry juice cocktail
2 teaspoons aromatic bitters (optional)
¾ cup sugar
30 inches stick cinnamon
1 tablespoon whole allspice
2 to 2½ cups dark rum (optional)

INSTRUCTIONS

Prepare Baked Apples in Brandy Sauce as directed. Meanwhile, stud oranges with cloves, if desired, then cut each orange into ¼"-thick slices; set aside. In an 8-quart Dutch oven stir together apple cider or juice, cranberry juice, and, if desired, aromatic bitters. Add oranges, sugar, stick cinnamon, and allspice. Bring just to a simmer; reduce heat. Cover and heat for 10 minutes. If desired, stir in dark rum and heat through. Transfer to large, heat-proof serving bowl. Add baked apples. If desired, stir in the 1 cup reserved brandy sauce from the apples. Makes about 21 (8-ounce) servings.

Baked Apples in Brandy Sauce: Core 8 small *apples* (about 2 pounds total). Peel off a strip around the top of each apple. Place the apples in a 13×9×2" baking dish; set aside.

For brandy sauce, in a small saucepan combine 1 cup packed *brown sugar,* ½ teaspoon *ground cinnamon,* ¼ teaspoon *ground nutmeg,* and ⅛ teaspoon *ground allspice.* Stir in 1 cup *brandy.* Carefully bring just to boiling over medium-low heat. Pour the brandy sauce over the apples. Cover with foil and bake in a 350° oven for 25 to 30 minutes or until the apples are just tender when gently tested with a fork.

Use a slotted spoon to remove the apples from the brandy sauce. Reserve 1 cup of the brandy sauce for the wassail. Or, serve apples with sauce as a dessert in individual dessert bowls. Makes 8 servings.

SPRINGERLE

Shown on page 148.

YOU WILL NEED

½ teaspoon baker's ammonia
   (hartshorn powder)*
2 tablespoons milk
6 large eggs
6 cups sifted powdered sugar
½ cup unsalted butter, softened
½ teaspoon salt
½ teaspoon anise or lemon oil*
10 to 10½ cups sifted cake flour
Food colors (optional)

INSTRUCTIONS

If not already powdered, crush baker's ammonia with a rolling pin. Dissolve in milk in a small bowl; let stand for 1 hour. Let eggs stand at room temperature for 30 minutes. In a large bowl of a freestanding electric mixer, beat eggs until thick and lemon-color, about 5 minutes. Gradually beat in powdered sugar until creamy and smooth. Add butter and beat again until creamy. Add dissolved baker's ammonia, salt, and anise or lemon oil; beat to mix. Gradually beat in as much flour as you can with mixer. Stir in enough remaining flour to make a stiff dough. Cut off pieces of dough and knead on a floured work surface until dough is stiff enough to roll out and hold the design of the springerle mold. Roll out on a lightly floured board with a floured rolling pin to ¼" thickness. Press design on dough with a floured springerle mold. Cut cookies apart using a floured knife or cookie cutter. Cover with a kitchen towel; leave on work surface overnight.

The next day, bake cookies on greased baking sheets in a 325° oven until barely golden on the bottom, about 10 to 12 minutes. Cool on wire

racks. Cookies may be decorated with food colors or edible paints. Store in tightly covered containers and allow to mellow a week before serving. Makes about three dozen 3½" cookies. Yield depends on molds used.

Note: This recipe can be made using 1½ teaspoons baking powder in place of the milk and the baker's ammonia and using anise extract instead of anise oil. However, the cookies will not be as delicately textured and the anise flavor not quite as rich. If using baking powder, add it with the salt to the batter. Baker's ammonia (also known as hartshorn powder) is a compound once used as a leavening agent; it is available at pharmacies.

SPICED WHOLE WHEAT COOKIES
Shown on page 149.

YOU WILL NEED
⅓ cup margarine or butter
⅓ cup shortening
1 cup all-purpose flour
1 cup whole wheat flour
¾ cup sugar
1 egg
1 tablespoon milk
1 teaspoon baking powder
¾ teaspoon ground cinnamon
⅛ teaspoon ground nutmeg
⅛ teaspoon ground allspice or cloves
1 teaspoon vanilla
Dash salt
Powdered Sugar Icing (see page 52)

INSTRUCTIONS
In a large mixing bowl beat the margarine or butter and shortening with an electric mixer on medium to high speed about 30 seconds or until softened. Add the all-purpose flour,

sugar, egg, milk, baking powder, cinnamon, nutmeg, allspice, vanilla, and salt. Beat until thoroughly combined, scraping the sides of the bowl occasionally. Beat or stir in the whole wheat flour. Divide the dough in half. Cover and chill about 3 hours or until easy to handle.

On a lightly floured surface, roll each half of the dough to a ⅛" thickness. Using 2 to 3" cookie cutters, cut the dough into desired shapes. Place 1" apart on an ungreased cookie sheet.

Bake in a 375° oven for 7 to 8 minutes or until the bottoms are light brown and the edges are firm. Cool on the cookie sheet for 1 minute. Remove the cookies and cool on a wire rack. Spread or pipe icing on cookies. Makes 36 to 48 cookies.

GINGER KIDS
Shown on page 149.

YOU WILL NEED
½ cup margarine or butter
2½ cups all-purpose flour
½ cup sugar
½ cup molasses
1 egg
1 teaspoon baking soda
1 teaspoon ground ginger
½ teaspoon ground cinnamon
½ teaspoon ground cloves
4 ounces vanilla-flavored candy coating, chopped (⅔ cup)
1 tablespoon shortening
⅔ cup semisweet chocolate pieces
1 tablespoon shortening
Powdered Sugar Icing (see page 52)

INSTRUCTIONS
In a large mixing bowl beat the margarine or butter with an electric mixer on medium to high speed about

30 seconds or until softened. Add about *half* of the flour and all of the sugar, molasses, egg, baking soda, ginger, cinnamon, and cloves. Beat until thoroughly combined, scraping the sides of the bowl occasionally. Beat or stir in the remaining flour. Divide the dough in half. Cover and chill about 3 hours or until the dough is easy to handle.

Grease a cookie sheet, then set it aside. On a lightly floured surface, roll each half of the dough to a ⅛" thickness. Using 3 to 4" people-shaped cookie cutters, cut the dough into shapes. Place 1" apart on the prepared cookie sheet. Bake in a 375° oven for 5 to 6 minutes or until the edges are firm. Cool the cookies on the cookie sheet for 1 minute. Transfer the cookies to a wire rack.

In a small heavy saucepan heat and stir the vanilla coating and 1 tablespoon shortening over low heat until melted. In another saucepan heat and stir the chocolate pieces and the remaining 1 tablespoon shortening over low heat until melted. Dip the hands, feet, and tops of the heads of the cookies in either the vanilla or chocolate mixture. Place on a wire rack until set. If desired, dip cookies again in the contrasting mixture; place on a wire rack until set. Decorate with icing. Makes about 36 cookies.

153

RIBBON CANDY

Shown on page 150.

YOU WILL NEED

3 cups sugar

1 cup light corn syrup

¼ cup water

6 to 8 drops peppermint oil or cinnamon oil

¼ teaspoon red paste food coloring

¼ teaspoon green paste food coloring

2 pairs white cotton work gloves

INSTRUCTIONS

Butter 3 shallow baking pans; set aside. Butter sides of 3-quart saucepan. In saucepan combine sugar, corn syrup, and water. Cook over medium-high heat to boiling, stirring constantly with wooden spoon to dissolve sugar, about 5 minutes. Avoid splashing mixture on sides of pan. Carefully clip candy thermometer to side of pan. Cook over medium heat, stirring occasionally, until thermometer registers 280°, soft-crack stage, about 20 minutes. Remove from heat; stir in peppermint or cinnamon oil.

Pour about two-thirds of mixture into one buttered pan. Pour half of remaining candy into a warm small saucepan. Add red coloring to this portion and pour into another buttered pan. Add green coloring to remaining portion in 3-quart saucepan. Pour into remaining buttered pan.

Let candy cool slightly, 3 to 5 minutes for larger, uncolored portion, 1 to 2 minutes for smaller, red and green portions. As edges cool, lift and fold edges to center with metal spatula. (If candy is too warm, it will stick to spatula.) When red and green candy can be rolled into balls with spatula, they are ready for shaping.

With gloved hands, pull and twist red candy until light in color, 2 to 3 minutes. Shape into 6" rope. Place in one of the buttered pans and keep warm in 200° oven. Repeat with green portion. At the same time, have second person pull uncolored portion until white. Shape into 6" rope.

Place white rope in center of one of the buttered baking sheets; place one colored rope on each side of white rope. Press all 3 ropes together to form a single flat log. Working quickly, have one person stretch one end of striped candy log lengthwise, working to other end until ribbon narrows to about 1" wide. Have second person immediately follow first person and turn ribbon onto one edge and fold accordion-style to make ribbon shape; break off in 6" lengths. If candy hardens too much, return to oven 3 to 5 minutes to soften. Makes 2 pounds.

CRYSTAL CANDY

Shown on page 150.

YOU WILL NEED

2 cups sugar

1 cup light corn syrup

½ cup water

¼ teaspoon desired food coloring

Few drops oil of cinnamon, oil of peppermint, or oil of wintergreen

INSTRUCTIONS

Line 8×8×2" baking pan with foil, extending foil over edges of pan. Butter foil; set pan aside. Butter sides of heavy 3-quart saucepan. In saucepan combine sugar, corn syrup, and water. Cook over medium-high heat to boiling, about 5 minutes, stirring constantly with wooden spoon to dissolve sugar. Avoid splashing mixture on sides of pan. Carefully clip candy thermometer to side of pan. Cook over medium heat, stirring occasionally, until the thermometer registers 280°, soft-crack stage, 20 to 25 minutes. Mixture should boil at a moderate, steady rate over the entire surface. Remove saucepan from heat; remove thermometer from saucepan.

Quickly stir in the desired food coloring and flavoring. Immediately pour the mixture into the prepared pan. Let stand 5 to 10 minutes or until a film forms over surface of candy.

Using broad spatula, begin marking candy by gently pressing a line across the surface, ½ " from one edge of pan. Do not break through film on surface. Repeat pressing, ½" along other 3 edges of pan, intersecting lines at corners to form squares. (If candy does not hold shape, it is not cool enough. Let stand a few minutes; start again.)

Continue marking lines along all sides, ½" apart, until you reach center. Retrace lines, pressing spatula deeper but not breaking film on surface. Repeat until spatula can be pressed to bottom along all lines. Cool completely. Use foil to lift candy out of pan; break into squares. Store covered. Makes about 1½ pounds.

To make molded candies, oil hard candy molds. Quickly pour the hot mixture into molds. Cool 10 minutes or until the candies can be removed. Cool completely.

RUM AND EGGNOG CAKES

Shown on page 151.

YOU WILL NEED

2¼ cups all-purpose flour

2 teaspoons baking powder

¾ teaspoon ground nutmeg

1 cup diced mixed candied fruits and peels

½ cup golden raisins

½ cup chopped pecans

2 tablespoons all-purpose flour

1½ cups butter (no substitutes), softened

1 cup sugar

3 eggs

1¼ cups dairy eggnog or reduced-fat dairy eggnog

1 to 1½ cups rum or 1 to 1½ cups orange juice plus ½ teaspoon rum extract

Eggnog Glaze

Candied cherries (optional)

INSTRUCTIONS

Grease and flour twelve 1-cup miniature fluted tube pans or one 10" (12-cup) fluted tube pan. Stir together the 2¼ cups flour, baking powder, and nutmeg in a bowl; set aside. Toss together candied fruits, raisins, pecans, and the 2 tablespoons flour; set aside.

Beat the butter in a mixing bowl with an electric mixer on medium speed for 30 seconds. Slowly add the sugar, beating until light and fluffy. Add eggs, one at a time, beating 1 minute after each addition. Add the flour mixture and eggnog alternately to egg mixture, beating on low speed after each addition until combined. (Do not overbeat.) Stir in ¼ cup of the rum or ¼ cup of the orange juice and rum extract. Fold in the fruit mixture. Pour the batter into the prepared pan(s).

Bake in a 350° oven until a toothpick inserted near center comes out clean, allowing 30 minutes for small pans or 55 to 60 minutes for large pan. Cool in pan(s) on a wire rack for 10 minutes for small pans or 15 minutes for large pan. Remove the cake(s) from the pan(s); cool completely on wire rack.

Poke holes in cake(s) with a toothpick. Soak 100-percent-cotton cheesecloth with rum or orange juice, using 1 cup of the rum or juice for small cakes and ½ cup of the rum or juice for the large cake. Wrap cake(s) in rum- or orange juice-moistened cheesecloth. Wrap tightly in foil or seal in plastic storage bags. Store cake(s) in the freezer or in the refrigerator for 1 to 2 days to mellow flavors. After 1 day, drizzle with the remaining ¼ cup of the rum or orange juice. Rewrap for another day, or serve. Drizzle with Eggnog Glaze; let dry about an hour before serving. Garnish with candied cherries, if desired. Makes 24 to 30 servings.

EGGNOG GLAZE

YOU WILL NEED

1 cup sifted powdered sugar

1 tablespoon dairy eggnog

1 tablespoon light corn syrup

½ teaspoon light rum or ¼ teaspoon rum extract

INSTRUCTIONS

Stir together sifted powdered sugar, 1 tablespoon dairy eggnog, light-color corn syrup, and light rum or rum extract. Add additional eggnog, one teaspoon at a time, until icing is of glazing consistency.

CRAFTING BASICS

CROCHET

Chain One Stitch

Make a slipknot about 4" from the end of the yarn and slip the loop onto the crochet hook. Weave the yarn loosely under the pinkie, over the ring finger, under the third finger, and over the index finger of your left hand; grasp the tail of the yarn between the thumb and third finger. Holding the hook (with the slipknot on it) in your right hand, slip it under the yarn, and then use the hook to pull it through the loop to complete one chain stitch. Continue chain-stitching the desired number of stitches to make a foundation chain.

Single Crochet

Step 1: At the beginning of a row, insert your crochet hook into the second chain from the hook.

Steps 2 and 3: Slip the hook under the yarn, and then use the hook to pull it through the chain. This is called "yarn over" (or "yarn over hook") and is abbreviated as "yo." Notice that there are two loops on the hook.

Steps 4 and 5: Yarn over again, and then pull the loop completely through the two loops on the hook. You have just completed a single crochet. To work the next single crochet, insert your hook into the next chain, and repeat steps 2–5.

Double Crochet

Step 1: At the beginning of a row, slip the hook under the yarn (yarn over), and insert the hook into the fourth chain from the hook.

Step 2: Yarn over again, and pull the loop through the stitch. There are three loops on the hook.

Step 3: Yarn over, and pull the loop completely through the first two loops on the hook. Notice that two loops remain on the hook.

Step 4 and 5: Yarn over once more, and pull the loop through the remaining two loops on the hook. One loop remains on the hook. You have

just completed a double crochet. To work the next double crochet, yarn over and insert your hook into the next chain; repeat steps 2-5.

Slip Stitch

Step 1: Insert your hook into a stitch. Yarn over, and pull the yarn through the stitch and through the loop on the hook. You've completed a slip stitch.

CROSS-STITCH

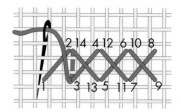

Basic Cross-Stitch

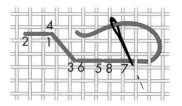

Backstitch

TRANSFERRING PATTERNS

Transferring a Pattern onto Fabric

1. Use an iron-on transfer pen with dark ink color for light-colored fabrics and white ink  for dark fabrics. Unless the pattern is printed in reverse, trace it with a pencil onto tracing paper, flip it over, and trace it with an iron-on transfer pen.

2. Position the tracing paper ink side down on your fabric. Using a hot iron without steam,  press on top of the paper to transfer the design.

Transferring a Pattern onto Wood

1. Duplicate the pattern by placing tracing paper over the design and tracing over it with pencil.

2. Transfer the design to the project surface by taping down the traced pattern. Place transfer paper under the pattern, and trace over it again with a stylus or pencil.

PAINTING

Stencilling

1. Dip the bristle tips of your dry stencil brush into the paint. Tap off most of the paint on a paper towel.

2. Apply the paint to the surface by pouncing the bristle tips up and down to  create a fuzzy or textured look.

Shading and Highlighting

1. Select your main color, such as red, and use it to base-coat the surface. Apply your paint with  the largest brush that will fit the design area.

2. Shade with a darker color, using the float-ing technique. Shading makes an area appear to  recede, separating it from the surrounding color.

3. Highlight your work by floating a lighter color on the design. High-lighting makes 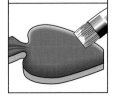 an area appear more prominent, adding dimension.

STITCHES

Blanket Stitch

French Knot

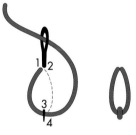

Lazy-Daisy

Running Stitch

Satin Stitch

Stem or Outline Stitch

SOURCES

Look for supplies to make our projects at arts, crafts, fabric, and needlecrafts stores, or contact these companies for more information.

CRAFTS

American Art Clay Company (Rub 'n Buff),
4717 W. 16th St., Indianapolis, IN 46222; 317/244-6871.

Binney and Smith (Crayola Modeling Magic),
1100 Church Ln., Easton, PA 18042; 800/272-9652.

Decorator & Craft Corp. (papier mâché boxes),
428 S. Zelta St., Wichita, KS 67207; 316/685-6265.

Hot Potatoes (rubber stamps),
2805 Columbine Pl., Nashville, TN 37204; www.hotpotatoes.com, 615/269-8002.

Krylon (spray sealer),
101 Prospect Ave. N.E., Cleveland, OH 44115; 800/457-9566.

Polyform Products, (Sculpey modeling compound),
1901 Estes, Elk Grove Village, IL 60007; www.sculpey.com.

Beacon Adhesives (Hold the Foam adhesive),
301 Wagaraw Rd, Hawthorne, NJ 07506; 800/865-7238.

Walnut Hollow (wood products),
1409 State Rd. 23, Dodgeville, WI 53533; 800/950-2112.

Wilton Industries (cake and candy making supplies),
2240 W. 75th St., Woodridge, IL 60517; 630/963-7100

PAINTING

DecoArt (paint),
P.O. Box 386, Stanford, KY 40484; 800/367-3047.

Delta Technical Coatings (paint),
2550 Pellissier Place, Whittier, CA 90601-1505; 800/423-4135.

Duncan Enterprises (Aleene's and Tulip paint products),
5673 E. Shields Ave., Fresno, CA 93727; 559/291-4444.

Plaid Enterprises (FolkArt paint),
P.O. Box 2835, Norcross, GA 30091; 800/842-4197.

NEEDLEWORK

Anchor (embroidery floss),
Consumer Services Dept., P.O. Box 27067, Greenville, SC 29616; www.coatsandclark.com.

DMC (embroidery floss),
10 Port Kearny, S. Kearny, NJ 07032; 973/589-0606.

Lion Brand Yarns,
34 W 15th St., New York, NY 10011; 212/243-8995.

Yarn Tree Designs (perforated paper),
117 Alexander St., P.O. Box 724, Ames, IA 50010; www.yarntree.com, 800/247-3952.

Wichelt Imports (embroidery fabrics),
Embroidery Services Department,
P.O. Box 139,
Stoddard, WI 54658.

Better Homes and Gardens ®

CHRISTMAS FROM THE HEART.

VOLUME NO. 9

EDITOR-IN-CHIEF **Beverly Rivers**
CREATIVE DIRECTOR **Daniel Masini**
CHRISTMAS FROM THE HEART EDITOR **Ann Blevins**
CRAFTS GROUP EDITOR **Eve Mahr**
ASSOCIATE ART DIRECTOR **Melissa Gansen Beauchamp**
EDITORIAL COORDINATOR **Carol Moorlach**
CONTRIBUTING WRITERS **Jil Severson and Rhonda Matus**
CONTRIBUTING GRAPHIC DESIGNER **Glenda Aldrich**
CONTRIBUTING ILLUSTRATORS
**Glenda Aldrich, Marcia Cameron, Barbara J. Gordon,
Chris Neubauer Graphics, and Carson Ode**
CONTRIBUTING PHOTO STYLISTS **Lenny Houtz, Patrick Lose,
and Laura Holtorf Collins**

PUBLISHING DIRECTOR **William R. Reed**
PUBLISHER **Maureen Ruth**
MARKETING MANAGER **Dale Engelken**
PROMOTION SUPERVISOR **Merri Moser**
BUSINESS MANAGER **Cathy Bellis**
PRODUCTION DIRECTOR **Douglas M. Johnston**
PRODUCTION MANAGER **Pam Kvitne**
ASSISTANT PREPRESS MANAGER **Marjorie J. Schenkelberg**

VICE PRESIDENT, PUBLISHING DIRECTOR **Jerry Ward**

Meredith CORPORATION

CHAIRMAN AND CEO **William T. Kerr**

CHAIRMAN OF THE EXECUTIVE COMMITTEE **E.T. Meredith III**

MEREDITH PUBLISHING GROUP
PUBLISHING GROUP PRESIDENT **Christopher M. Little**

For book editorial questions, write:
Better Homes and Gardens®, Christmas From the Heart®
1716 Locust St., Des Moines, IA 50309-3023

Member
HOBBY INDUSTRY
ASSOCIATION

ISSN: 1081-4698
ISBN: 0-696 20899-7

CONTRIBUTING PHOTOGRAPHERS

Craig Anderson: Page 81.
Marcia Cameron: Pages 70 (top),
73, 84 (top), 108-109, 112, 119, 121,
126, 133.
Mike Dieter: Pages 47 (top), 151, 155.
Hopkins Associates: Pages 54–55,
59, 110.
John Kane: Page 56.
Jim Krantz: Pages 47–50.
Pete Krumhardt: Page 57, 58.
Scott Little: Pages 6, 15, 33, 36, 61,
67, 69, 70 (bottom), 74, 75 (bottom),
76, 78, 82. 88, 103, 104, 122, 128,
134, 138, 141, 142, 143, 145 (top),
148, 152.
Andy Lyons: Pages 30.
Perry Struse: Pages 6–7, 8–13, 18,
22–23, 24–28, 30–31, 32, 34-35,
60–61, 62–66, 68, 75 (top), 78-79, 80,
83, 94–95, 96–101, 102–103 (top),
111, 118–119, 120, 123, 124–125,
134–135, 136–137, 139, 140, 144,
145 (bottom), 150.
Steve Struse: Pages 14, 38, 43, 84
(bottom), 95, 105, 106, 133 (bottom).

Contributing Artists: Britanie Breeden,
Josh Breeden, Marcus Breeden, Macaully
Breeden, Alyssa Witt, and Michael Witt.

Cover Photograph: Perry Struse